# The Zen of Executive Presence

# The Zen of Executive Presence

## Build Your Business Success
### Through Strategic Image Management

## David A. McKnight

Printed in the United States of America.

The Zen of Executive Presence
Build Your Business Success Through Strategic Image Management

ISBN (Trade Paperback)     978-0-9896551-0-1
ISBN (Kindle eBook)        978-0-9896551-1-8
ISBN (iPad/Nook eBook)  978-0-9896551-2-5

Cover design by Sam Chae, Cleverbird Creative, Inc.
Images by David A. McKnight, DAMstyle Inc.

# Contents

# Dedication

To my mother for always being an inspiration and best friend, no matter what.

To my family and friends for encouraging me to pursue my dreams.

To my former colleagues at Deloitte Consulting for enabling me to pursue my passion and my profession.

To my clients for trusting me to help them get closer to their personal and professional goals with image and style.

# Why Image Matters

## CHAPTER ONE

Before we discuss why image matters, let's identify what image is. Many people assume that *image* refers solely to our personal appearance — to our fashion sense, grooming habits and physical fitness. Thanks to this assumption, fueled by various TV makeover shows, people tend to equate image management with fashion consulting, with the makeovers seen on programs such as *Queer Eye for the Straight Guy* or *What Not to Wear*.

In reality, physical appearance is only one component of our image. It is one of a myriad of ways that we express *who we are* (or think we are) to the world.

Your image is *your* concept of yourself. This concept is developed in your mind, projected into the physical universe and, once the concept is "out there," interpreted and acted upon by the people around you.

Image is the collection of external messages that we communicate (intentionally or not) about our inner selves. We communicate these messages not just through our appearance, but also through our actions, our speech and our lifestyle.

Everything we say and do communicates something about us. Everything contributes to our external image. Short of never being born, there is no way to *avoid* projecting an image. Once we accept this fact, we have two choices:

1.  We can attempt to manage other people's perceptions of who we are, so these perceptions will more accurately align with our self-image.

2.  We can do nothing, or even adopt the contrarian view that "image doesn't matter," that image is something that concerns only "superficial people," and if someone can't intuit who we are "on the inside," we want nothing to do with them.

Unsurprisingly, I strongly advise you to make the first choice and avoid the second, because the second attitude is nothing more than a *denial of reality*, however inconvenient that reality may be. In the real world, humans are hard-wired by their evolutionary history to perform instant assessments of other people — of their personalities, temperaments and intentions, not to mention their suitability as mates.

Before the invention of language, a small tribe of peaceful hunter-gatherers had no way of knowing whether a band of stick-and-spear-toting strangers was interested in trade or in kidnapping the women and killing the men. Waiting until those strangers made their intentions known could be a disastrous choice. Therefore, we humans learned to interpret facial expressions and body language. We learned to interpret gestures and movements for signs of hostility versus friendliness; honesty versus deception.

Yes, such assessments can be hasty. Yes, these assessments are based on "surface" cues, including appearance, speech and non-verbal signals. No, these assessments are not always accurate.

However, because image assessment has sometimes meant the difference between life and death, people continue to spontaneously and subconsciously respond to outward images in much the same way that their ancestors did.

Image *is* superficial — it is superficial by definition. The very term "image" refers to the mental formations that arise when we interpret data from our sense organs. But just because something is superficial doesn't mean it isn't valuable.

Our self-image reflects what we believe to be true about ourselves. It is greatly informed by our experiences and the social constructs in our surroundings. Our outer image is formed from this inner image — from our inner thoughts, experiences and values.

It's fair to assume that a Brooklyn hipster will have a different set of values and beliefs than a Utah Mormon. This is why, during the casting of reality TV shows like *The Real World* on MTV, the directors look for people ("characters") with vastly different backgrounds and appearances. The directors know that different external images probably reflect different internal values, and that these internal differences will eventually surface in the form of personality conflicts.

# Image Can Make or Break a Career

For better or worse, image really does matter. Your image produces first impressions, and first impressions contribute to people's *lasting* impressions. Because of this, your cultivation and development of the proper image is critical to your career enhancement and your professional advancement — the focus of this book.

Although image matters in both your personal and professional lives, *managing* your image matters most to your career. If the sixty-something CEO of a Fortune 500 company wears a beehive hairdo, biker jacket and pink hot pants on the weekends, the damage will probably be limited to a few giggles from passersby. If she brings that image with her to the boardroom, though, she might lose her job (unless most of the board members are fans of the 1980s band The B52s).

Make no mistake. I'm not arguing that you must shed your personal tastes and adopt "Stepford Wife" conformity when it comes to your dress, speech and behavior. I'm merely advising that you express your individuality within the boundaries of what's considered appropriate in particular situations, organizations and professions.

Whether you're conscious of it or not, the image you project makes a big difference to your professional life. Image matters because it shapes people's views of how you're likely to behave in different contexts, as well as your level of competence and intelligence — both IQ and EQ (emotional intelligence).

One research study revealed that when we first meet people, we make eleven decisions about them within the span of just seven seconds:

- Economic level: *where* they fit into society; how rich or poor they are;

- Educational level: how intelligent they are, as well as the probable extent of their schooling — e.g., high school diploma, undergraduate degree, graduate degree;

- Their honesty and credibility;

- Their trustworthiness;

- Their level of sophistication;

- Their sexual orientation, desirability and availability;

- Their level of success;

- Their political views;

- Their value orientation: whether or not you share the same ethics and values;

- Ethnic origin;

- Social desirability: how much you'd like the person as a friend.

The reasons for these instant judgments are rooted in our "genetic history as human beings — most of which has been spent swinging around in trees and eating one another ... [For] our own protection, we [need] to sum up strangers very quickly to ensure our survival; are they friend or foe or perhaps lunch or dinner?"[1]

Some research suggests that job interviewers make up their minds about candidates within the first four minutes. Other studies have determined that it takes just *one tenth of a second* to make an image judgment.[2] In other words, not only do we *not* get a second chance to make a first impression, we barely have a chance to manage the first impression — unless we've cultivated and refined that impression in advance.

Appearance discrimination is pervasive in the workplace, and it's actually increasing because (among other things) it's so difficult to prove. Bias against overweight people is a real phenomenon in corporate America, which is one reason Weight Watchers has seen an influx of unemployed people in recent years.

In *Beauty, Gender and Stereotypes: Evidence from Laboratory Experiments*[3], researchers found a strong positive correlation between higher incomes and higher perceived attractiveness. Another study, conducted at the University of Florida and the University of North Carolina, discovered that tall people earn considerably more money throughout their careers than shorter people.

---

1   Eggert, Max A, "Body Language for Business." New York: Skyhorse Publishing, 2012.
2   Ibid.
3   Andreoni, James and Petrie, Ragan, "Beauty, Gender and Stereotypes: Evidence from Laboratory Experiments," Journal of Economic Psychology, 29 (2008) 73–93.

# The Zen of Executive Presence

Although self-image is created in our minds — by our concept of who we truly are — external image is shaped by societal pressures and popular culture.

In other words, our external image is constructed from elements that we *can* and *cannot* see; that we *can* and *cannot* control. More important, our external image may contain elements that we can't even define.

Consider the definitions of "charisma" from *Webster's New Universal Unabridged Dictionary*: 1) A divinely conferred gift or power; 2) A spiritual power or personal quality that gives an individual influence or authority over large numbers of people; 3) The special virtue of an office, function, position, etc., that confers or is thought to confer on the person holding it an unusual ability for leadership worthiness of veneration, or the like."

If you've ever met someone with a charismatic personality, you will probably agree that these definitions don't even come close to describing the "vibes" exuded by someone with real charisma — the charm and power that is hypnotic/magnetic/persuasive — that a charismatic person exerts on other people.

A colleague who met former New York Governor Mario Cuomo described the politician's charisma in this way: "I was physically *punched* by his presence. He generated a 'personality wave' that nearly knocked me off my feet — a wave of confidence, conviction, determination, persuasion and sincerity. If he had commanded me to quit my reporting job to become a hairdresser, I probably would have. Before the meeting, I had never experienced charisma. I still can't convey what it's like to meet someone with a charismatic personality, except to say that charisma is a powerful, *physical* presence generated by the person who owns it."

Alfred Hitchcock referred to this kind of superstar charisma as "It."

Movie stars have "It." Garden-variety actors don't.

I call this executive presence.

Like charisma, executive presence is impossible to define. Words cannot adequately or accurately convey the reality of the phenomenon. Because we humans (most of us) do not possess telepathic abilities, we cannot instill in others precisely the same feelings and thoughts that we experience in response to a particular person or event. I can describe the most beautiful sunset I ever saw, but I can't place into your mind *precisely* the same feelings and thoughts I experience. Even if you were sitting next to me, watching the same sunset, you and I would have different experiences.

We all experience different thoughts and feelings when we encounter the same images, and most of us can't explain *why* we react in the ways we do. Unless the beholder of an image has a deep background in image consulting, branding, fashion, communications, body language or psychology, she will recognize a "good" or a "bad" personal image when she sees it, but she won't be able to pinpoint *why* the image produced a positive or a negative reaction. It's similar to how the average moviegoer responds after the show. She can't always identify the reasons a movie *worked* or *didn't work*. She merely *knows* that she liked it, hated it, or was indifferent.

Obviously, this presents a problem. How can I help you develop executive presence if I can't explain what it is?

I wrestled with this dilemma for a while — until a colleague recommended that I read *The Way of Zen* by Alan Watts. By the time I finished reading the book, the solution had become obvious. Like a Zen Master, I decided to point the way to the ultimate goal, even though I couldn't describe what the goal looks like. In traditional Buddhist art, the Buddha is often depicted pointing toward the moon. The Buddha represents the teacher, the moon the ultimate goal (Enlightenment), and his pointing finger depicts the methods by which the student will be trained to reach the goal.

I came to see a parallel between the indescribable state of Buddhist Enlightenment and the indescribable state of executive presence.

I realized that executive presence is a little like the concept of Enlightenment — a state of mind in which the student has "awakened" to Universal Truths. Because these Truths can't be fully explained using language, Zen masters don't try to define Enlightenment. Instead, they set the students on the right path, so they can discover Enlightenment for themselves.

The Zen master can't explain what Nirvana *is*, but he can explain what Nirvana is *not*, and this keeps students from wandering off course. By the same token, I can't tell you what executive presence *is*, but I can tell you what it is *not*.

So my mission is to help you discover for yourself what executive presence is. I'll simply point you toward a professional image — a professional presence — to increase your chances for career success.

First, I'll describe the attributes and traits common to people with executive presence. Then I'll offer strategies to help you build and manage a professional presence and (with luck) an executive presence.

What I will *not do* is recommend an instant "makeover."

I disagree with the premise behind makeovers. In my experience, makeovers rarely work. In fact, a quickie makeover can inflict more harm than good.

One of the biggest dangers of the makeover is that the consultant or stylist will superimpose an inappropriate image on the victim — I mean *client*. In many cases, the client will discard the new image (or certain components of it). In other cases, the client will continue to pound her "round self" into the "square hole," generating an image that strikes most observers as artificial or phony. Unless the consultant takes the time to properly and thoroughly assess the person's current image, and develop a new image that reflects the person's *authentic self*, most clients will abandon the made-over image.

Image makeovers are like liposuction. If ten people receive liposuction, five of them will gain back the weight within a year. The problem is the same in image consulting because the concept is the same — changing someone at the surface doesn't change the underlying habits, motivations and personality traits that produced the problems. You can change someone's surface image overnight, but you cannot change the person's lifestyle, personality, eating habits, values and beliefs overnight.

## Image + Identity = Brand

Your image plus your identity equals your brand.

Your brand is the collection of images that you present to the world over time. It is a continuum of images reflecting your authentic self.

If I come to work one day looking clean and well-dressed, but show up the next day unshaven and unkempt, my brand will not be consistent. However, if I am consistently punctual, ethical, well-dressed, well-groomed and friendly, colleagues and clients will come to identify me with those attributes. This will create a consistent brand. Friendly, punctual and well-dressed becomes my brand.

A positive brand can't be established or enhanced overnight. But even the most carefully crafted and well-loved brand can be destroyed in an instant.

While campaigns are trying to sell their candidates like commodities, voters shop for the most appealing brand. Thus when voters go to the polls, they do not simply show their preference but also take ownership of their candidate. They deepen the connection to the brand.

So what happens when Mitt Romney speaks bluntly about the so-called 47 percent; or your governor or senator has an extramarital affair; or your state senator misappropriates money that was meant for a nonprofit? After incidents like these, voters decide fairly quickly whether or not the candidate's brand is irreparably damaged. After all, when voters make political or policy choices, they are often asked to defend those choices among family, friends or co-workers. When your candidate does or says something indefensible, you don't want to be stuck trying to defend it. You're more likely to rethink your preference or choose not to participate.[4]

Consider the case of Tiger Woods: Tiger created a highly-prized brand based on an image that personified what Americans most admire in their athletes — talent, hard work

---

4    Basil Smikle, "Contradicting a Carefully Built Brand." *The New York Times*, September 18, 2012.

and achievement harnessed to humility and "squeaky clean" values. This brand helped him earn millions of dollars in product endorsements. But Tiger destroyed the brand overnight when it was revealed that he was a serial adulterer. Tarnished almost beyond redemption, Tiger's brand will never be what it was — no matter how hard his marketing team tries to rehabilitate it.

More recently in the news, cooking show maven Paula Deen self-imploded after news of her racist comments hit the media; her not-quite-sincere apologies crumbled her cooking empire. Random House's Ballantine Books canceled her publishing contract, joining up with the Food Network, Smithfield, Wal-Mart, and a collection of other companies in ending business relationships with the queen of Southern cooking.

We *all* have an image.

We *all* have a brand.

The key is not just to establish an image or brand, but also to *manage it.*

Each and every day, employees are hired and fired, promoted and demoted, rewarded and punished, and friended or unfriended based on perceptions about their brands. Although it's true that smart, hard-working employees get laid off in tough economic times, the first to be fired are often those perceived as lackluster. All things being equal, management usually fires the "slackers" and the "second-stringers" first; not the "premium brands." The latter are terminated only when the firm's circumstances become desperate.

Because our brand is established over many decades, enhancing the brand requires that we carefully assess what is working and what is not. It also requires us to perform a thorough assessment of where we are today, where we want to go, and how to get from here to there. Long-term image enhancement cannot be achieved through instant makeovers, because it takes time and careful effort to fashion an image that "syncs" with your authentic self.

# Image Enhancement Starts with Synchronization

The image you present to the world must be rooted in your internal identity, and the internal and external must synchronize with each other. If your image truly stems from your internal identity, it will project authenticity. This authenticity will be inviting to others. They will sense that you are honest, real and sincere. If you are comfortable with your true self, others will be comfortable with you, too.

When there's a conflict between your internal and external images, it's often felt by those with whom you interact. Regardless of your superficial makeover efforts, people will subconsciously realize that you're hiding something or not projecting your authentic self.

The problems experienced by Mitt Romney during the 2012 presidential campaign stemmed not so much from a poorly crafted brand, but from his continual "gaffes" — remarks that were incongruent with his brand. Romney's campaign managers sought to project an image of competence, confidence and decisiveness. His brand was that of the "turn-around specialist" — the savvy business executive who knew how to reboot the economy and revitalize the middle class. When a videotaped speech was revealed, in which Romney labeled half of Americans as "moochers" who refused to take personal responsibility, the revelation produced "cognitive dissonance" in many voters. It created a disconnect between a carefully crafted brand and the truth — or what many people perceived as the truth about Romney's real views. Even those people who agreed with his clandestinely videotaped statements considered the remarks a sign of incompetence — and arrogance. And if Romney's brand didn't represent competence, what *did* it stand for?

Few brands can withstand such cognitive dissonance.

Recognizing that the internal influences the external, I begin my image-consulting process by helping clients discover their true personalities. Personality is a simple, easily identifiable variable in the complex matrix of image-generating factors. Personality can give us a quick glimpse into who someone really is.

I start with a proven tool for assessing personality, asking clients to identify a list of traits that they (or others) would use to describe them. These traits are categorized by seven Universal Styles™ — a system created by Alyce Parsons in 1990. Once the Universal Style™ is identified and the client's personality is better understood, I match their personality type to more appropriate wardrobe choices. At a minimum, this helps ensure that the person's outward appearance is more congruent with her personality and internal image.

For instance, if someone has a spontaneous, adventurous and imaginative personality, but she works in corporate finance, there may not be many opportunities to showcase her internal creative self through professional attire. And this conflict between the inner self and the outer self may result in "career fatigue" because her authentic self is constrained by her business environment and workplace role. I try to bridge such gaps by synchronizing the client's wardrobe with her personality — without going overboard.

Wardrobe and personality are not the only two image projectors that may be out of sync. Sometimes, a person's actions may not be in harmony with his appearance, or the way he lives at home may be incongruous with the image he presents at work. To have a completely fulfilling life, it's important to properly align all aspects of your image. This is an evolutionary process; it cannot be done overnight or over the weekend. Often, it takes many months to fully align the internal with the external image.

As young professionals move up the career ladder, the concept of image synchronization becomes more and more critical. Greater attention must be paid to the way you look, act and communicate to ensure there is alignment between who you are and the image you project.

Everyone can project a more positive image.

Everyone can develop a winning brand.

Everyone can develop a professional presence and, in many instances, an executive presence.

However, this image (your brand) must be consistent with who you really are as a human being. The public image must be based on the *best possible version of you.*

Step #1 in building a professional presence — and eventually, an executive presence — is to take a few moments to answer the questions that follow.

# Assessment Exercise

1. What words do others use to describe you?

2. What words do you think accurately describe you?

3. Are there conflicts between your view and others' views?

4. What are the strengths of your current brand?

5. What are the areas you need to improve?

6. What are the things you can begin doing now to enhance your current brand?

# The Attributes
# of Executive Presence

## CHAPTER TWO

N o one can capture exactly what executive presence is, but we can describe some key attributes and traits exhibited by people who have "It." These include:

| | | |
|---|---|---|
| Authenticity | Courage | Intelligence |
| Candor | Determination | Passion |
| Clarity | Humility | Poise |
| Compassion | Humor | Sincerity |
| Confidence | Insight | |

As a "laundry list," these character and personality traits are of limited value. However, they do provide a suitable launch pad — a finger pointing toward the moon — for determining what executive presence is and what it is not.

# A Rare Breed

People who project executive presence are a rare and memorable breed.

In the course of daily business activities and client interactions, leaders with executive presence stand out from their competitors by demonstrating knowledge, expertise, ease and genuineness. They are interesting people who are always prepared with topics to discuss. What's more, they are not afraid to raise difficult issues. Instead of viewing sensitive topics as potential landmines, these leaders tackle these issues to build better relationships with colleagues, superiors and — most of all — customers and clients.

No doubt, you've occasionally met people like this in the course of your professional life — dynamic "thought leaders" who have the ability to broach delicate subjects and make courageous (but compassionate) arguments without alienating or embarrassing everyone in the room. In fact, the person's sincerity, humility and good humor may have induced collective laughter or even sighs of relief. You may have thought, "It's about time someone addressed this topic head on, instead of letting it fester beneath the surface."

By contrast, I'm sure you know at least one person who produces the opposite reaction — the eccentric uncle or sibling who routinely says things (usually at holiday dinners) that are so inappropriate that everyone secretly wishes they could suffocate the offender with a plastic dry-cleaning bag.

Leaders with executive presence demonstrate honesty, integrity and the ability to continually enrich a conversation, even when moving beyond their areas of expertise. They are also skilled at listening and asking questions. Colleagues and clients immediately recognize the crispness of their thinking. These leaders never "sell." Instead, they view every interaction as an opportunity to build a more personal relationship with the client.

Finally, leaders with executive presence are never dependent on PowerPoint presentations or printed handouts to drive their arguments or make important points. Often, they will open a presentation or discussion at the head of a bare table, without materials, and produce supporting documents only when they are relevant to the conversation.

Unfortunately, most managers do not possess executive presence. As leaders, they are merely adequate.

The adequate leader follows a transactional approach to communications and personal interactions. She presents her arguments, looks for opportunities to close the deals, attempts to close them, and continues attempts to close them even after her comments are no longer welcome.

The adequate leader demonstrates solid technical expertise in her chosen field, but avoids discussions that extend beyond those areas. In addition, adequate leaders shy away from discussing difficult or sensitive topics, especially when their opinions and expertise might be construed as challenging the clients' views. Adequate leaders get the job done in a workmanlike fashion, but they don't create lasting impressions or lasting relationships.

Beneath adequate leaders we find "unreliable leaders." Like the adequate group, these people follow a transactional approach to interactions. Sometimes the approach works; sometimes it falls flat. By and large, their interactions leave people doubting their knowledge, expertise and genuineness. In fact, these interactions often cause prospects or clients to seek a second opinion from someone who's likely to provide more insight, meaning they often turn to competitors.

Of course, things could always be worse. Someone could be viewed as a leader who is *unworthy of trust*.

People who fall into the final category — "self-interested" leaders — tend to approach every business interaction in the same way. They *want something* from the other person, and they won't stop pounding away until they get that something. Borrowing a page from David Mamet's play *Glengarry Glen Ross*, self-interested managers follow the rule of **ABC** — **A**lways **B**e **C**losing. They're always trying to close deals without first gaining buy-in from co-workers and customers. They try to achieve their goals without first forming relationships based on trust and mutual respect. Their interactions leave clients not trusting them. As a result, most clients will refuse to work with them again.

The self-interested leader is personified by the slick scam artists depicted in *Glengarry Glen Ross*. This type of leader is seen as someone who cares only about himself, as someone with no moral compass, compassion, humility, sincerity or poise. In short, his image projects *none* of the traits that comprise executive presence.

## Executive Presence — Observable Behaviors

People with executive presence display a variety of behaviors. Despite this variety, however, all of these behaviors are congruent with the personality traits listed at the start of this chapter. For example, at no time does the leader with executive presence lapse into ego-fueled boasting or rude treatment of co-workers and subordinates. His very appearance is a silent but powerful indicator of his status in the corporate environment. Would you expect the CEO of a Fortune 500 company to be dressed in ripped jeans and a soiled T-shirt? No. He should be impeccably dressed in a finely tailored suit.

The man or woman who displays executive presence comes prepared for all interactions, adding value through something that is said or through thoughtful questions. This person does his homework before any and every meeting, presentation, phone call, email, tweet, client dinner and social event. The person with executive presence also:

- Starts client interactions with a clean desk, and focuses the conversation on what the client wants to talk about;

- Gets to know colleagues and clients personally, taking advantage of social settings to learn more about them;

- Is skilled at listening and asking thoughtful questions;

- Is thoughtful about her appearance in the context of the setting;

- Thinks carefully about the collateral materials to bring to a meeting, including business cards;

- Demonstrates appropriate etiquette in social interactions;

- Demonstrates confidence by not being afraid to ask tough questions or deal with challenging situations. Instead, the person views them as a way to strengthen relationships. Caveat: asking tough questions and broaching sensitive topics requires a great deal of finesse. There's a good reason most people shy away from tricky topics and sensitive issues;

- Makes effective use of time, attempting to add value and set precedents for future interactions by being memorable. If she has just 15 minutes with a CEO, she comes prepared with penetrating questions and insightful information;

- Is prepared to navigate through awkward moments with something to say, while also demonstrating confidence;

- Is aware of his own strengths, weaknesses AND the image he projects.

Conversely, someone who possesses executive presence does *not*:

- Remain silent during interactions or come unprepared. In very few situations, it is possible to remain silent and still command a room;

- Display quirky habits such as tapping a pencil or fiddling with hair;

- Dress inappropriately for the audience or setting, or fail to consider the image that he wants to project through his clothing, accessories and grooming;

- Fail to demonstrate an understanding of the client's situation or the purpose of the interaction, particularly when using collateral materials in a presentation;

- Display nervousness and unease when her clients want to talk about topics outside of her expertise;

- Assume that his title or business card will project the necessary aura of expertise and authority on his behalf;

- Squander time, leaving clients with no desire for future interactions;

- Make awkward moments even more awkward;

- Demonstrate that he is oblivious to his own strengths, weaknesses and image;

- Demonstrate unease and lack of confidence in interactions beyond technical presentations — e.g., social events, hallway/elevator conversations, or dealings with less senior employees of the client such as support and security staff.

# Developing Executive Presence

Enhancing your image, including executive presence, requires time. It requires a plan.

It starts with awareness — with recognizing (or being helped to recognize) that you need to change your image. From there, the process requires that you accept and understand the image components that need to change. In the realm of image consulting, denial is the enemy.

**Denial is the Number One cause of failure.**

Resistance to change is the second leading cause of failure. Changing your image requires a sincere desire to change

— and then you must take actionable steps to implement the change. Once your image has been enhanced, it is time to practice management and maintenance. You'll need to follow strategies that will help you maintain the modified image and keep you from backsliding into bad habits.

I'll provide more detail about the steps to image enhancement in later chapters. I'll discuss wardrobe choices, verbal and non-verbal communication skills, business etiquette and other factors that will improve your professional presence. The elements that comprise professional presence are very teachable, including posture, body movements, gestures, facial expressions and eye communication, as well as proxemics (the difference between personal space, intimate space and social space).

Executive presence requires understanding and mastery of many "soft skills" — compassion, genuineness, authenticity, active listening, humor and humility. Some people are so focused on numbers and data that they ignore the soft skills, or even denigrate them. That's fine for some — these people tend to be just adequate leaders. However, if you want to be more than adequate, if you wish to develop executive presence, it's time to study the soft skills.

Former President Bill Clinton is a leader with unquestioned executive presence, which he demonstrated during his keynote speech at the 2012 Democratic National Convention. I strongly recommend that you watch this speech on YouTube. His performance was a *tour de force*. If you watch carefully, you can tick off every observable behavior associated with executive presence.

# What Executive Presence Is Not

Executive presence does not equal power.

It does not emanate from the title on a business card, the volume of someone's voice, the cost of his clothing, the location of his office or the size of his ego.

You can give someone authority over thousands of employees, pay him a seven-figure salary, and seat him behind a monolithic desk, but none of this will generate executive presence. In fact, these accoutrements might give people the impression that the executive has a "Napoleon Complex" — that he is overcompensating for a lack of executive presence by enveloping himself in the trappings of power.

Someone with executive presence is not necessarily the loudest in the group. In meetings, he may be "a man of few words," talking when he needs to talk, but making his points in a very concise manner. This person is a highly effective speaker and not just a "talker." Some of my junior colleagues have great presence, but little official power. Remember: *executive presence is a form of soft power*, title and rank notwithstanding.

Professional presence and executive presence *can be learned*. For most people, however, the attributes needed for executive presence are hiding in our "blind spots" — i.e., most people don't know which of their qualities contribute to or detract from executive presence. Without help, most of us will never recognize when we are creating executive presence or destroying it.

It is good to have a healthy ego, but having executive presence does not mean that you must exert the gravitational pull of the planet Jupiter — that everyone should revolve around you and your desires. You haven't established executive presence when people fall into your "orbit," agreeing with everything you say, kowtowing to your wishes and affirming your magnificence. On the contrary, the word "egotism" should never come to mind when thinking of someone who has executive presence.

Before I landed my first consulting job, I interviewed with a number of companies, including a small firm led by a hard-charging individual. This man personified almost every trait that *detracts* from executive presence. Within seconds, it was obvious that I had not been called in for a job interview. I had been summoned for an "audience" with his majesty. Because he had built his company from scratch on the back of some innovative ideas, he wanted everyone to bask in his radiant glory.

He boasted. He bragged. He asked me questions about him, his worldview and his organization — questions to which I couldn't possibly know the answers. The questions were not designed to elicit information about my skills and attitudes. They were his platforms for launching self-congratulatory speeches. They were designed to test my ability to flatter his ego. I'm not sure he even listened to my responses. In fact, the only time he "woke up" while I was speaking was when I said something he didn't like. He, in fact, did this several times. He asked questions about concepts and theories he had invented. He would then say, "What do you think?" If I didn't answer "correctly," he interrupted to tell me why I was wrong.

By comparison, I recently worked with a client who oozes executive presence. This gentleman conveys humor and humility, sincerity and real compassion for his colleagues and employees. While most clients ask, "How can I have more presence in a meeting?" this client wanted to help his *subordinates* project more presence, even if that meant tamping down his own presence so they could shine more brightly. He actually asked me, "How can I have less presence?"

This ex-football player knew that business success requires a team effort. He was concerned about his own presence, because whenever he entered a room, all of the focus and respect drained away from his subordinates. Whenever he was in the room, clients directed their questions to him and away from his managers. This is why he (initially) wanted to reduce his presence.

The irony here is that only a person who has executive presence would wish to sacrifice that power for the sake of his teammates. Only someone with genuine compassion and empathy would project that attitude. Someone without these beliefs and values will never acquire executive presence, no matter how many books he reads or how many consultants he hires.

Projecting the "right" image means projecting your authentic self, but if that authentic self is built on egotism and selfishness, you'll need to fix your authentic self before fixing your image. Put bluntly: applying lipstick to a pig produces a lipstick-wearing pig, not a handsome prince or a beautiful princess.

Executive presence is a competency that becomes increasingly important the higher you move up in an organization. It is less important for a working supervisor, but critical for a president or CEO. Presence is not about selling a business transaction or showcasing your knowledge, capabilities and skill-sets. It is about creating experiences for others that make them want to know more about you, your personal brand and your business. Someone with executive presence has the ability to connect threads of conversation and to quickly detect other people's interests, leadership styles and business needs. By doing this, the leader will earn the right to explore more meaningful and purposeful business relationships.

## The Goo

All leaders with executive presence also possess professional presence, but the reverse is not true.

The man or woman who displays *professional* presence has *acquired* the skills of dressing, communicating and behaving appropriately in a variety of situations. The person with *executive* presence has *mastered* these skills and abilities, adding so much charm and charisma into the mix that their image stands head and shoulders above other professionals. This person's image seems both magical and effortless. Because no "seams" are showing, you must scrutinize every facet of appearance, communication style and business etiquette to put your finger on why this person produces the effects that she does.

Like the Zen Buddhist who realizes Enlightenment, image mastery cannot be entirely taught. It cannot be entirely learned from a book. The person with executive presence must acquire *some* mastery through direct, intuitive experience.

In other words, to acquire executive presence, you must *experience* executive presence — if only for a moment. Once that moment occurs, you can capture, replicate and apply the experience for the rest of your professional life.

It's the old cliché of learning how to ride a bicycle. You can read a thousand books on how to ride a bicycle. You can start with training wheels. But you will never acquire mastery until you have the experience of riding a bicycle without training wheels.

My goal is to guide you on the right path until —
some day, at some revelatory moment — you experience what
it's like to project executive presence. At that point, you will
move beyond professional presence into the rarefied realm of
executive presence. In that instant, you will know at a deep level
what it means to exude something akin to "charisma." What's
more, you will quickly develop an intuitive knowledge of how
to keep projecting executive presence for the rest of your career.
As with a bicycle, once you learn to project executive presence,
you'll never forget.

This is the Zen paradox: in order to learn what an
indefinable something is, you must experience that indefinable
something. For that to happen, you must be "battle tested." As
George C. Scott said in the movie *Patton*, regarding whether or
not his soldiers would "chicken out" the first time they came
under enemy fire: "When you put your hand into a bunch of
goo that a moment before was your best friend's face ... you'll
know what to do."

It's time to put your hand in the goo.

# Assessment Exercise

1. Can you start a meeting with a client with a clean desk? Can you focus solely on what the client wants to talk about?

2. Do you get to know colleagues personally, learning more about them in social settings?

3. Do you pay attention to your appearance and modify it to match different settings or situations?

4. Do you carefully consider which collateral materials to bring to a meeting?

5. Think of examples of appropriate etiquette in different social interactions, or examples you've seen of inappropriate behavior. Do you monitor yours carefully to always maintain good etiquette?

# Professional Presence

## CHAPTER THREE

To develop executive presence, you must first develop (or enhance) your professional presence. Just as you can't learn to run without first learning to walk, you can't develop executive presence without acquiring professional presence.

Professionalism has no simple definition. What one company considers professional dress and comportment would be completely unacceptable at another. If a factory supervisor arrived on the floor of his plant wearing an Armani suit and sporting the vocabulary of an Ivy League professor, this image would instantly alienate him from many colleagues and subordinates. Conversely, if a Wall Street banker wore clip-on ties and corduroy jackets to client meetings, and took his clients to dinner at McDonald's, he'd be regarded as a social misfit (at best).

In general, companies select employees whose personal brands reflect the corporate brands. For our purposes, therefore, professionalism is the "image standard" that an organization expects of its employees and managers.

Professionalism is an extension of the brand promise of the organization. It includes the manners, etiquette, ethics, global business practices, self-presentation and the pride employees demonstrate every day in their appearance and interactions with others. To some degree, your personal brand must reflect the corporate brand from the very start (the corporate brand as interpreted by your peers and executives) or you wouldn't even land a job at that organization. Once you are hired, the corporate brand and corporate culture will continue to shape your personal brand for the duration. If your personal brand does not evolve in sync with the company's, your colleagues and superiors will eventually notice the "brand disconnect" and take appropriate action — usually unfavorable action.

## Perception Is Everything

Professional presence affects not only the workplace but also how clients, customers and other companies view you, your associates and your subordinates. It reinforces the image that others have of the company and everyone associated with it. For this reason, projecting a professional presence is vital to business survival, whether you are a small business owner, a corporate manager or a frontline employee. Professionalism produces trust among peers and customers, fostering an image of competence, confidence and reliability.

Like it or not, perception is everything in the business world. Unless you've developed the Zen-like ability to pierce the veil of everyday reality, and can immediately understand the intentions and motivations of everyone you encounter, your perceptions (short-term and long-term) are the only tools you have to guide your actions. If you enter a bank lobby and spot a man donning a ski mask and pulling a semi-automatic pistol from his pocket, your perception will be that the man is planning to rob the bank. While it is *possible* that you accidentally wandered onto a movie set, the only information given to you by your brain's analysis of sensory information (perception) is that you have stumbled into a dangerous situation, and you had better flee. Ignoring those perceptions would be unwise.

A less extreme example comes from a friend — a freelance writer. With limited time to service existing clients and pursue new business leads, George must rely on the images projected by prospective clients to qualify leads. Like every savvy businessperson, George must avoid devoting precious time to people who are unlikely to buy his services. This is an issue that every salesperson confronts on a daily basis.

Consciously and subconsciously, George evaluates each prospect's appearance, gestures, vocabulary, body language, and business etiquette — i.e., the professional presence — for clues to whether or not the person (and by inference, the organization that the person represents) is likely to buy.

In addition, he quickly assesses whether the prospect's account would prove profitable or unprofitable, pleasant or unpleasant. In short, he uses "image analysis" to determine if a prospect matches his *ideal client profile*. If the prospect seems to match his "unlikely to buy" or PITA (Pain In The Ass) profiles, he politely terminates the conversation at the earliest convenient moment.

"If someone telephones me," says George, "and this has happened *dozens* of times — and his first question is 'How much for a press kit?' then I know from experience that I'm probably not dealing with an ideal client. There is a 99 percent chance that I'm talking with someone who knows nothing about public relations or advertising. There is a 99 percent chance that the person won't know the difference between good public relations writing and something written by a kindergartener.

"How do I know that? Well, in my experience, a true professional *never* starts the conversation with 'Hey, how much for X?' He starts by introducing himself, his company and his goals, and then describes the project he wants to undertake. Timelines and prices are discussed later.

"When I first launched my business, I wasted hundreds of hours on prospects who weren't competent or even serious professionals — people who had just taken a seminar on how to make instant millions selling stuff on the Internet; people who wanted someone to slap together some web content for fifteen dollars.

"Eventually, I learned how to recognize the ideal clients and the not-so-ideal clients based on first impressions — from the images they projected.

"I've probably rejected some good prospects because they made poor first impressions, but overall, I'm happy to rely on first impressions — on what you'd call my 'gut instincts' of someone's professional presence. It has saved me *a lot* of time, and has helped me earn much more money than I otherwise would have."

Saving valuable time and earning money — these are the ultimate reasons that we feel more comfortable doing business with people who have professional presence, and why we avoid "unreliable" and "self-interested" people.

# Audience, Role, Environment and Occasion

I'm often asked, "How can I be authentically myself at work and yet be professional?" In a recent survey, more than 88 percent of respondents said that professionalism is related to the person, not to his or her position. Nearly 40 percent believe that Generation Y (the "Millennials" born between the late 1970s and early 2000s) have poor grammar skills; about 30 percent said Generation Y has a poor attitude, and 27 percent reported that Generation Y employees are "disrespectful and inconsiderate."[1]

These findings, while not as pronounced in other demographic groups, pose a substantial problem for managers. As the most visible examples of professional behavior in any workplace, managers set the tone in the organization by conducting themselves in a manner that either supports or detracts from professional presence. The burden is on managers to develop a work environment in which professionalism is modeled, valued and enforced. This is easier said than done, but with proper coaching, every person is capable of learning professional behavior.

Although some of the details that create professional presence will vary from company to company, professionalism can *always* be defined as appearances and behaviors that are appropriately matched to:

- Your audience;

- Your role vis-à-vis that audience;

---

1   Don E. Sears, "Gen Y Shows Lack of Professionalism at Work: Report," eWeek, October 28, 2010.

- The environment in which you are interacting;

- The specific occasion or circumstances.

# Adaptable Elements of Professional Presence

I am *not* suggesting that companies send only middle-aged Caucasian men to negotiate business deals with the Chinese. I'm merely pointing out that, just as every company has a different definition of professionalism, different cultures have different definitions of what makes someone more or less professional, and these definitions may be influenced (rightly or wrongly) by ethnicity, gender and/or physical appearance.

**Your Audience:** Are you in the company of clients or colleagues? Senior managers or support staff? People who earn six-figure incomes or individuals who can only dream of six-figure salaries? Will your audience be receptive to you and your views, or is it more likely that they'll be skeptical or even hostile? Is the audience composed of peers, subordinates, superiors, or a combination of these people? What are the audience demographics — e.g., average age, education levels, political leanings, and so forth?

Sometimes audience composition doesn't matter — for example, if you have assembled all of your employees in a room to announce generous Christmas bonuses. But sometimes audience demographics can be crucial, determining how much respect is given to company representatives. Like it or not, ethnic and gender biases still exist. In certain Asian countries, for example, I have noticed that Caucasian men are assumed to have higher status than African-American or Latino men, and that men are sometimes accorded more respect than women.

**Your Role:** Understand your role, and know what is appropriate for the role in terms of dress and communication style. If you are delivering a presentation to an audience of your peers, you have assumed the role of an authority figure — an expert. In this society, the rule of thumb is that authority figures dress "a notch above" their peers in order to convey that authority. Whether you wear a three-piece suit or a turtleneck sweater depends on the audience. If, during the course of your presentation, you want to relate more to your audience, you might take off your jacket and roll up your sleeves to indicate that you are "getting down to business now," and you and every audience member are now solving a problem together.

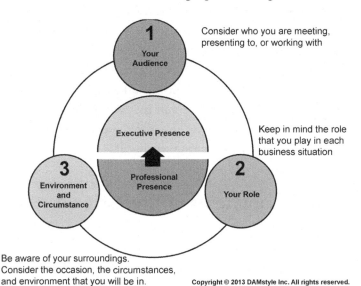

**Figure 1. Adaptable Elements of Professional Presence.**

**Environment:** Are you meeting with a team of financial services executives in the company's board room, or with a group of nurses in the hospital's lunch room? Are you on a factory floor or inside the CEO's well-appointed office? Are you in a casual dining restaurant or a white tablecloth establishment with a wine steward? *Understand your environment* at all times, and know what kind of dress standards and etiquette are required in that environment. It may be acceptable to chug a few beers with the CFO at the company picnic, but not at the black-tie fundraiser to which she invited you.

**Occasion:** Is the occasion formal or casual? Will the occasion involve business discussions or merely social pleasantries? Job interviews are occasions for which you always want to look your best. The potential employer should see you looking better than you'll ever look while working for the company. Job interviews are almost like wedding days if you consider how you should dress and comport yourself. Once you have established yourself at the company or with your client, you can "let your hair down" a little. Once your peers and superiors come to know (and presumably like) you as an individual, and not just as an employee, you can be a bit more relaxed and reveal your true authentic self.

## Four Components of Professional Presence

Collectively, these four components form the standards of professionalism at the core of executive presence — and all of these components are "controllable." With the right education, coaching and practice, you can improve each of these image aspects.

**Appearance:** This refers to the visual aspect of your professional image, from dressing to grooming to body language and even to your work environment.

**Communication Style:** This addresses effective communication as a professional, whether it's through oral, written or non-verbal methods.

**Business Etiquette:** This refers to actions and behavior protocols in business settings, ranging from networking events and in-house meetings to client meals.

**Online Presence:** This is the virtual aspect of your personal brand, and how it's affected by online activities.

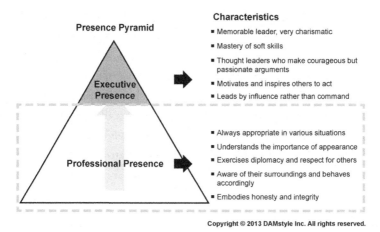

**Figure 2: Professional vs. Executive Presence.**

The remainder of this book focuses on the four major attributes — appearance, communication style, business etiquette and online presence — that comprise professional presence *and executive presence*. Based on these attributes, I'll walk you through strategies to build and manage a more professional image.

You already have an image — a personal brand. But you may have left key elements of your branding up to chance, or you are imitating role models whose attributes may be inappropriate because they do not reflect who *you* really are. I will offer you only the most fundamental tactics for enhancing these four elements. There are literally thousands of books and magazine articles that discuss image enhancement tactics regarding your appearance, communication styles, etc., so to repeat them here would be redundant. It would also require a much longer book — one the length of several Bibles. For that reason, I will largely focus on key strategies and leave the tactics to other book and magazine authors.

Because I don't know you as an individual, I can't offer advice to enhance your individual image. Makeovers rarely work because they rarely reflect the *individual's* needs. Most "one-size-fits-all" makeovers do not produce an authentic expression of the client. More often than not, the client is transformed into someone she is not. This is like painting over a beautifully inlaid parquet floor instead of giving the floor new luster to display its materials in the most flattering way.

# Assessment Exercise

1. Think about your dressing habits, your daily grooming. How could this be improved?

2. What changes could you make to your work environment to better reflect your style and your professionalism?

3. On a scale of 1 to 10, how would you rate your communication effectiveness? How could it be better?

4. What changes do you make to your actions or behavior in different business settings?

5. Consider your online presence. Do you maintain consistency of professionalism online? How do you think others see you?

# Assess Your Current Image

## CHAPTER FOUR

I f we could really see ourselves as others see us, none of us would have image "blind spots." Without a professional third-party evaluation, however, few people have the skills to objectively evaluate their image and the impressions it makes on other people. The gap between our own self-image and the image others have of us creates these blind spots. Therefore, the first step in enhancing your image is to assess your current image by obtaining a third-party evaluation.

Ideally, this assessment will be conducted by a professional — an experienced consultant who specializes in image, wardrobe, color, speech, body language, social and business etiquette, or a combination of these. If you cannot locate or cannot afford such a consultant, it is better to self-assess than to do nothing.

You *could* enlist the help of trusted friends, acquaintances, relatives and colleagues, as long as they are willing to be honest, and as long as they aren't the actual *source* of certain problems.

This could prove difficult. Friends, colleagues, and others we've known for a long time might find it impossible to be objective. Some will project their own tastes and prejudices on you. And because many people live in "opinion bubbles," associating mostly (or exclusively) with people who share the same tastes, styles and worldviews, it's possible that you have problems created (or enabled) by friends, relatives and colleagues.

We all have an image. We all have a brand. That image is the sum total of messages we communicate about ourselves, which others then interpret to form mental impressions of who we are. As we form relationships with people, their perceptions of us often change. Someone's first impression might be "He's short" or "He's opinionated" or "He's kind of a geek" — and "therefore, he must also be X, Y and Z." As you reveal more about yourself over time, though, the image others have of you will naturally become deeper and more complex. Normally, the outer image will come to more accurately reflect the inner you. However, unless you're an exceptionally aware *and* self-aware individual, you will probably never know what most people think of you.

Even if you request honest feedback, many people will offer comments that are incomplete or even disingenuous for fear of violating the societal convention that states: *If you can't say something nice, don't say anything at all.* You won't know anything about your brand unless someone points it out to you — unless someone educates you on what your brand is and what it means, describing how your identity combines with your image. Few people are so self-aware that they can obtain a "30,000-foot view" of themselves. Few ever achieve "image enlightenment" on their own. "No wonder I didn't get that promotion! I've been projecting Image X instead of Image Y!"

I see this every day in the business world and with my clients. People ask, "Why can't I get more clients? Why can't I get a salary raise? Why does this competitor always beat me?" It's obvious to *me* what they should be doing, but not to *them*. They have no clue what they are doing wrong. By the time they become my clients, these people know they're doing something wrong. They have realized that they need help. But they rarely know *what* to do. That's when they turn to an expert.

## Strategic vs. Tactical Help

What kind of person approaches me about image consulting? What kinds of problems do they usually describe? Do people wake up one morning and say, "Holy crap, I'm projecting a terrible image!" Did someone just comment on their poor grammar or wardrobe for the first time, causing them to suddenly see the need for change?

Yes, that *does* occasionally happen. More often than not, however, the person has just identified certain image-problem symptoms and approached me to help develop enhancement strategies (as opposed to makeover tactics). People who ask for tactical assistance usually email to say, "I need help with my wardrobe. I don't know how to accessorize and match things." People who approach me for *strategic* help usually email to say, "I can't seem to get second dates" or "I'm always overlooked for promotions at work. What am I doing wrong?" Some people contact me with "I recently got a divorce, so I'm looking to start over. I want to change my image. I think I need a new hairstyle. I think I need a new look, but I don't know where to start." The last two scenarios are more strategic. These people are thinking about their whole image instead of specific improvements to their wardrobe or hairstyle.

In general, significant personal and career problems are symptomatic of significant image problems — problems that will require extensive image consulting. Conversely, minor personal and career problems are usually indicative of an image that just needs some "tweaking" rather than an overhaul.

For example, I once worked with a woman who had recently lost about 200 pounds. All she really needed was a new wardrobe, because she was unaccustomed to choosing clothing that revealed or complimented her body. She was a pretty woman with a nice figure, but even after losing the weight, she was still buying clothes that were too big — she was accustomed to trying to camouflage her shape. My mission was to teach her how to embrace and flatter her new figure. I helped recondition her self-image, reinforcing in her mind that she had a nice body to show off, and that it was okay to wear things contoured to her body. Today, she looks amazing.

On the other hand, I've worked with clients who had no idea what they were doing wrong. They just knew that something wasn't working because they weren't achieving good results in certain areas of their lives. They weren't landing jobs after attending dozens of interviews — interviews they considered "successes." They weren't being asked to spearhead projects and weren't receiving promotions or sufficient recognition for their efforts.

Among my clients, the most common blind spots are related to wardrobe and grooming. They usually involve clothes that are out of date or ill-fitting. Or the problem involves a hair color or style that, while flattering to the celebrity who wears it in a magazine, isn't a good match with the client's skin tone, hair type or facial shape.

The most common blind spot with communications and etiquette is ignorance. The client is simply unaware of behavioral standards and best practices. For example, did you know that your choice of pen can either enhance or diminish your professional presence? It's true. During a business meeting, the saleswoman who plucks a stylish fountain pen from her notebook is more likely to make a favorable impression than the woman who uses a disposable ballpoint. It's a tiny and seemingly insignificant detail, but included along with every other image detail, it makes an impression on others.

Strategic or tactical, the effect produced by most blind spots is an *inconsistent image*. By itself, one poor clothing choice is not a disaster. It is the cumulative effect caused by a continuum of poor choices that leads to eventual disaster — like the would-be executive who comes to work looking like a million bucks one day, but looks like a vagrant the next day. What would you think of someone who dressed so inconsistently? That he's unreliable? That he cares about his appearance on some days and not others? That he isn't competent to dress himself? That he goes shopping while he's drunk? How does the inconsistent image shape your opinion of him as a person or an employee?

When assessing your current image, pay special attention to inconsistencies, however small. As an example, consider Rosie O'Donnell — specifically her smile. In every photo I've ever seen of her, the comedian looks like she's ready to bite the head off the next autograph seeker who interrupts her lunch. That's because her smile appears forced and phony — it looks completely inauthentic. Ms. O'Donnell's smile has two attributes that most smiles share: her mouth is open and the teeth are revealed. Aside from that, her facial expressions resemble those of a vicious tigress baring her teeth.

A similar observation was made about Governor Mitt Romney's laugh. An analysis of his laugh by James Lipton, host of *Inside the Actor's Studio*, pointed out inconsistencies between the image Romney wished to project and the image that many voters perceived:

> *Why doesn't Mr. Romney's audience believe him? Perhaps it starts with his laugh, a device he employs at odd moments and in a most peculiar way. (The public thinks that crying is the acid test of the actor, but in fact "laughing" is much harder — and Mr. Romney hasn't mastered it.)*

Listen to his laugh. It resembles the flat "Ha! Ha! Ha!" that appears in comic-strip dialogue balloons. But worse — far worse — it is mirthless. Mr. Romney expects us to be amused, *although he himself is not amused.* Freeze the frame, cover the bottom of his face with your hand, and study his eyes. There's no pleasure there, no amusement. Genuine laughter is triggered only by — and is completely dependent on — shared perception. That's why we say we "get" a joke.[1]

I don't mean to keep picking on Governor Romney, but the public image that he and his advisors "managed" during the 2012 campaign is an excellent case study in what *not* to do.

## The Four Cs

Professional presence is composed of four factors, which I call the "Four Cs":

- Comportment

- Confidence

---

1   James Lipton, "How to Act Human: Advice for Mitt Romney *from Inside the Actors Studio.*" *New York Magazine*, May 12, 2012.

- Competence

- Consistency

The person with professional presence consistently comports himself in ways considered appropriate to every audience, role, environment and occasion, while simultaneously projecting confidence and competence. During a job interview, for example, the person who possesses the Four Cs demonstrates competence by pointing to "transferable skills" when he's asked why he would be a good fit, despite his lack of industry experience. "You have a philosophy and sociology dual major, but this is an investment bank. How does that translate?" To this, the candidate might point to relevant skills that his education provided vis-à-vis buyer psychology and client relationships. If he has prepared for such a question — as he should have — he can also display confidence and personality by telling jokes or making a few witty remarks.

In terms of comportment, he will know to lean forward (slightly) to demonstrate interest in what the interviewer is saying. He will sometimes mirror the body language of the interviewer, and he will maintain appropriate levels of eye contact. He comes across as friendly and relaxed, and speaks in a conversational tone. He will not seem nervous, self-conscious or rehearsed — to the point where it becomes obvious that he has memorized a list of HR-approved clichés, with which he repeatedly interrupts the interviewer before the questions have even been asked. These behaviors demonstrate the very opposite of confidence, competence and proper comportment. Good comportment is built on an understanding of appropriate behavior and social deftness. It can't be taught entirely from a book, but must be exercised in the real world to become ingrained. The same thing goes for competence, confidence and consistency. Unless you're a natural when it comes to the Four Cs, you will make "youthful mistakes." However, by learning something about image, image enhancement and professional presence, those mistakes will serve as valuable career-building lessons. At a minimum, you will never repeat those mistakes.

I know people who have made "every mistake in the book" when it comes to projecting a poor image in the workplace, especially during job interviews. One of my friends launched his career at a very prestigious company but, when the time came for him to move on, it took him a year (and two dozen interviews) to find another job. During this period, he just couldn't understand why nobody would hire him — until one interviewer finally explained some facts of life. Whenever my friend was asked to explain why he wanted to leave such a prestigious company, he would absolutely trash his supervisors in a speech that sometimes lasted 15 minutes.

Halfway through this speech, one interviewer finally stopped him. He said, "Why don't you just say that your opportunities for advancement were limited? It's never a good idea to bash your former employer. It will lead people to think that *you* were the problem, not the employer." My friend was shocked. He had not realized what kind of image his response had been projecting. When he was next asked (at another interview) why he wanted to leave his current position, he repeated what the previous interviewer had told him — and he got the job.

This is why *awareness* is so critical to the image enhancement process — awareness generated from a third party's feedback. My friend knew he was doing something wrong during those interviews, but until he met that one candid interviewer, nobody would tell him what the "something wrong" was. Nobody would tell him that his comportment was unprofessional in his one response to a single but all-important question.

## Symptoms

Determining if you need to change your image can be as difficult as assessing your image — because image is a taboo topic for many people and companies. Trying to help someone overcome an image problem is frequently interpreted as an insult or a faux pas — akin to standing up during a business meeting to announce that the new client stinks of body odor. This is why many people go through their lives without making much-needed changes. Like the emperor with no clothes, they are unaware that they need improvement, and nobody wants to point out their flaws. A partner at one company went ten years without any feedback on his weight problem. When someone finally had the courage to offer helpful feedback, he was grateful for the critique, and now wishes that someone had pointed out this flaw much earlier.

NOTE: Be *very* careful before offering an image critique, and don't try to help everyone. Pointing out some people's flaws may expose you to harsh criticism — if not retaliation — because some people are overly sensitive about their images. They might interpret your comments as insults or even as attempts to bully them.

A few years ago, UBS attempted to force professional standards "out of the closet" by issuing guidelines for professional dress and conduct. Unfortunately, the bank's approach was so heavy-handed, and produced such a backlash from employees, that the company quickly scrapped its how-to manual. UBS management thought they were helping promote higher professional standards by offering definitions of professional comportment and attire, but the initiative was interpreted as an insult by many workers. Management's heart was in the right place, but their brains were not. They failed to broach the issue with the necessary tact and sensitivity. They also failed to consider that their employees are not clueless idiots whose manners had to be micro-managed. Was it really necessary, for example, that the manual include a warning about consuming garlic at client luncheons?

Companies should provide high-level guidelines centered on broad categories of behavior. There should be no need to micro-manage every detail of employees' dress and behavior. If there *is* such a need, then there's obviously a problem with the recruitment process. If HR does its job properly, it will screen out candidates who think it is acceptable to wear shorts and T-shirts in the office. If a company is recruiting the right talent, it won't have to tell employees to shower, shave and comb their hair before coming to work. (Unfortunately, there's a bit of a Catch-22 at play: because fewer parents and schools teach children good manners and enforce strict dress codes, it has become increasingly difficult for HR departments to recruit "the right sort of talent.") Corporate efforts to establish and enforce professional standards are needed now more than ever, but the UBS fiasco demonstrates that the efforts must be handled with finesse.

I worked with a junior colleague whose behavior was typical of today's younger generation. She's a beautiful woman, quite voluptuous. She knew it, and she flaunted it at every opportunity. She wore very tight clothing. Her cleavage was always protruding over her blouse. At the same time, she was intelligent and very good at her job. She simply needed to be pulled aside for a chat — which I did. "It's important to be aware of the messages we communicate through the clothing we wear," I said. "Unfortunately, sometimes the messages we send are unintentional and unbeknownst to us. In some instances, what we choose to wear may be considered distracting by others."

As a manager, it's important to have awareness-building conversations. But before initiating these conversations, *be sure to consult with the HR department first* to learn what you should and should *not* say or do, or you could be headed for trouble. For example: though I critiqued my junior colleague's wardrobe choices without repercussions, the same comments might be misconstrued (big time!) if they came from the mouth of another male *supervisor*. A woman might decide that the comments were a subtle form of sexual harassment by reading between the lines — e.g., "You're *too* sexy for this office, babe, and you're driving me wild."

Don't walk into a legal and/or human resources catastrophe. Talk to an HR representative before blurting out something you'll come to regret. Among other things, consider differences in gender, ethnicity and status before determining what should be said to the employee (if anything) and who should be the one to say it. As a co-worker, I was able to say things to my friend and colleague that a boss might not get away with. In some cases, it's better for critiques and advice to come from other members of the person's peer/ethnic/gender group than from bosses or "outsiders."

For better or for worse, most people never get an intervention when it comes to their image. Instead, they notice symptoms of an image problem, and then seek help in locating the causes of the symptoms. One common complaint is completing multiple job interviews without receiving an offer. The same may be true of your love life. You go out every weekend hoping to attract a new romantic interest, but the relationships always fizzle within a few weeks, days, or even hours. Maybe you're a very attractive person — all your friends tell you so — but whenever you go out, you never attract the right person (or even attract the wrong people). Why?

Recognizing that something's wrong is the first step in image enhancement. Making excuses merely contributes to the problem. "It's the economy" is not a valid excuse for repeatedly failing to seal the deal after multiple job interviews. While the economy is a reasonable explanation for a dearth of job opportunities, it cannot explain why you fail to land a job after repeated interviews with firms that are actually hiring.

Most often, the symptoms of an image problem take the form of failures at significant professional goals, despite considerable effort. If you analyze the situation, you will detect patterns. You will notice, for example, that every job interview seems to start well. You answer questions articulately and thoroughly, but halfway through the process, the interviewer's mood darkens and she hastens to end the interview. Or maybe you receive good performance reviews, but you're constantly passed over for promotions.

If you're not sure whether your image needs improvement, look for particular symptoms and patterns that keep cropping up in your professional life — e.g., you complete promising job interviews, but never get call-backs or job offers; perhaps conversations with colleagues or dates usually fizzle out. You are frequently excluded from informal conversations or formal meetings with powerful inner circles at your place of work; your relationships with co-workers terminate at the entrance to the building (you're never invited out for drinks after work). These could be symptoms of an image problem that is affecting or will in the future negatively affect your career.

# Build a Personal Image Management Team

Building your own personal image management (PIM) team is the first step in developing a polished image — a positive image that gets you noticed. Your team will be composed of experts who will help you achieve your image goals and objectives. These goals are not limited to just your physical appearance; they also relate to your behavior, communication style and personal space.

Your PIM team may include, but does not have to be limited to, a personal shopper, personal trainer, nutritionist, dentist, dermatologist, esthetician, and hair stylist or barber. The primary goal of these experts is to help you look and feel your best, because when you look and feel your best, you will behave at your best.

Some of these advisors are well-equipped to discuss image tactics; others can discuss long-term strategies as well as tactics. Collectively — if not individually — these experts can help you maximize your potential, so you communicate clear and consistent messages to the world through the image you project.

Of course, perfecting an image requires that you first envision a new image — one that the experts will help you project. A good start toward envisioning a new image is to first identify the things you *don't* want. For example, you don't want others to view you as aloof and stand-offish. Instead, you want them to regard you as warm and genuine. Performing exercises that document everything you *don't* want to project, as well as what you *do* want to project, will increase your clarity about the image you want to develop and/or refine. From there, you can adopt tactics that are suitable to projecting that image.

Among other things, I teach clients to assess the energy of the clothing in their wardrobes. For instance, while working with one client on her wardrobe, she held up a pair of old pants, asking for an opinion. Seeing that they were dated and not very stylish, I turned the question back on her. "What do *you* think about the pants?" She proceeded to complain about the pants, saying they made her look fat; she didn't like the noise they made when she walked. I said, "Just listen to how you described those pants. You have nothing positive to say about them. Every comment was negative."

We must listen to the "energy" of our clothes. If we don't feel good when we put something on, or if it makes us unhappy, those feelings will be present throughout the day and our vibrations will be low. This is why I often launch the image enhancement process with the client's wardrobe. Wardrobe is the most visible and obvious expression of the person's current image.

# Assessment Exercise

1. Write down what you don't want your image to be. Draw a line down the middle of the paper and then write down what you do want your image to be.

2. Look at your wardrobe and evaluate the energy of each garment. Rate each item on a scale of 1 to 5, where 5 means that you love it, 3 means you're indifferent, and 1 means you hate the thought of wearing it. You can come up with your average energy level of your closet by averaging the scores together. Or you can average the energy level of each garment group type — for example, you may find that you love your shirts and tops, but you really don't like your pants selection.

# Your Visual Image

## CHAPTER 5

No matter how often we're told not to "judge a book by its cover," we do. We make judgments about other people based on their appearance, especially our first impressions of that appearance. We make assumptions about people's personalities, temperaments, backgrounds and intentions based on height and weight, race and gender, clothing, accessories and hairstyles. It's an instinctive response that can't be turned off. Although we know that first impressions of a visual image can be misleading, we can't command our minds to cease making judgments. We can't because these judgments are instinctual — a deeply ingrained part of our evolutionary psychology.

Until recently, "judging a book by its cover" was an essential human survival tool — one that helped our ancestors avoid danger and ensure survival of the species. Before the advent of 20th century medical tests, there was no way for a man to know, in advance, if a potential mate could bear children. Instead, he had to rely on physical attributes that, more often than not, indicated that a woman was fertile. These surface attributes included youth, facial symmetry and smooth, blemish-free skin. Conversely, women judged men as potential fathers and protectors based on physical characteristics that included height, weight and strength — factors that also contributed to the man's status in the tribe or extended family.

At the subconscious level, men and women continue to use these ancient criteria to evaluate the desirability of a potential date or mate. In the workplace, we use these and other criteria to evaluate the competence and intelligence of our subordinates, colleagues and managers. Based on visual appearance, as well as verbal and non-verbal signals, we also determine whether a particular job candidate or co-worker is a potential ally or rival.

## Wardrobe Engineering

Appearance makes a powerful and instant impression. In fact, the research of Dr. Albert Mehrabian suggests that physical appearance counts for 55 percent of a first impression. The *content* of your speech — what you actually say when meeting someone — represents just 7 percent of the first impression. Fortunately, visual image is controllable. Even someone who hasn't been blessed with many natural assets can significantly enhance his image, at least in the professional arena, by re-engineering his wardrobe. Before doing this, of course, you must understand the effect that various wardrobe choices have on the typical viewer *in the context of different professional environments.* On any given day, at any given time, it is important to design a visual image for yourself that projects a professional presence. Remember, however, that the definition of professional presence varies. It depends on:

- The occasion;

- The environment;

- The audience;

- Your role within or related to the audience.

In the context of the workplace, your clothing effectively constitutes a uniform. Even if you are not one of the millions of Americans who actually wears a uniform mandated by the company, your wardrobe should reflect the image that your organization wishes to project. Because your personal brand is, by default, an extension of your company's brand, your wardrobe choices, hairstyle and grooming must sync with what the company wants to project in the context of the environments, occasions, audiences and roles in which you find yourself. You can't possibly project a professional presence if your appearance contradicts the company's branding efforts.

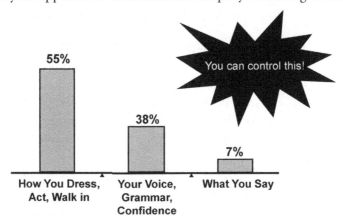

Source: Mehrabian, Albert (1971). Silent Messages (1st ed.). Belmont, CA: Wadsworth. ISBN 0-534-00910-7

**Figure 3: Visual image is controllable.**

You must always be aware of your projected image, meaning that you must acquire a basic knowledge of what is and what is not appropriate dress and grooming in every circumstance you're likely to encounter. Though most of us acquire some understanding of what to wear and when, we may not know *why* certain choices are considered appropriate. A superficial understanding of why certain wardrobe choices are right or wrong can cause trouble if we enter uncharted territory — when we find ourselves in gray zones where there is no clear-cut good or bad choice.

If you are delivering a formal presentation in an auditorium before an audience of industry experts or potential clients, your choices will be limited and relatively easy to make. You already know that:

- The occasion is formal;

- The environment is formal;

- Your audience will be dressed conservatively;

- The role of a presenter is that of "an authority figure," and in American society, an authority figure is expected to dress a notch above the audience. If everyone in the audience will be wearing suits and ties, you could wear a three-piece suit, or at least wear a suit that appears to be of high quality.

On the other hand, I recently consulted with a woman who worked with a Canadian hospital at which the average employee earns just $9.50 an hour. This woman had great style. When I met her, she was wearing Christian Louboutin shoes with red bottoms, and a stunning suit. She also wears Burberry and Dolce & Gabbana. However, when she meets with the clients, she tones down her high fashion sense. Although she still projects the image of a well-dressed authority figure, she wears clothing and accessories that are less expensive — items that the average hospital employee could afford. This allows her to project expertise and authority without placing too much distance between herself and the clients. She wants to comes across as "one of them," not someone who hails from a higher socio-economic class — someone who might not be able to relate to the client's problems and challenges.

## The ABCs of Visual Image

Within the image industry, a common tool used by image consultants is the notion of the ABCs of image — your appearance, behavior and communication.

Anyone can learn to improve appearance by:

- Accentuating the positives;

- Camouflaging the negatives;

- Creating optical balance and symmetry.

Beauty may be in the eye of the beholder, but modern science says that *symmetrical* faces and bodies are what people find attractive. Young or old, European, Asian or African, people find symmetrical bodies and faces more appealing than asymmetrical ones. Believe it or not, a significant number of people have features that are *not* 100 percent symmetrical, though most observers are not conscious of the asymmetry. Instead, casual observers tend to find people with symmetrical faces more attractive than those slightly asymmetrical features — without knowing why. The reason people are drawn to symmetry is simple: it's a sign of robust health and, in women, the ability to bear children. Poor health produces asymmetries — small imperfections that humans instinctively find less desirable.

Another visual cue of good health is clear, smooth skin free of blemishes, as well as healthy white teeth. In addition to being unattractive in and of themselves, crooked and missing teeth contribute to asymmetries of the face and jawline.

Women with a 70 percent waist-to-hip ratio are considered the most attractive — e.g., a woman with 34-inch hips and a waist measuring approximately 24 inches. This ideal feminine shape is commonly known as the "hourglass figure." As mentioned earlier, taller men earn more money on average than their shorter peers, and men who are considered "very masculine" are also well-muscled and have pronounced (often square) jawlines.

An image consultant can help you identify any asymmetries and assist you in assembling a wardrobe that will accentuate your strengths and camouflage your weaknesses. Almost all of us have both strengths and weaknesses because it is rare for someone to have both a "perfect" face and "perfect" body — to be born a modern-day Aphrodite or Adonis.

Refining your image is largely a matter of choosing clothing in the styles, colors and fits that will best accentuate *your* strengths, camouflage *your* weaknesses and achieve balance and symmetry for *you* — not the model wearing them on the magazine cover or online catalog. When I do this for my clients, I am not guided by any hard and fast rules — in my experience, hard and fast rules are made to be broken! There are, however, a few style guidelines that apply to almost everyone on the planet.

For example, I'm often asked by women, "Should I pull my hair back or wear it down?" There is no "one-size-fits-all" answer to that question. The answer depends entirely on the woman, her hairstyle, and her professional situation. With hair, my one biggest guideline is that it should never become a distraction for either the woman or her audience. If her bangs are so close to her eyes that her eyelashes are brushing against the bangs every time she blinks, the bangs should be shortened.

I recently watched Dr. Phil interview a young man whose bangs were epoxied over one eye. I have no idea what the interview was about because I spent the entire 15 minutes wondering what kind of gel he used to keep his hair in place, and if it interfered with his driving. It was so distracting that I could not pay attention to anything else.

The same goes for hair that you must constantly push back behind your ear because you need a haircut — or hair that keeps falling over your face. When your hair becomes a distraction or a chore, you need to do something about it. When you're speaking to an audience, you want them focused on your words, not your hair.

When assembling a professional wardrobe, my Number One guideline is to choose clothing that fits into one or more universally accepted styles of professional dress — i.e., into one or more of the *Seven Universal Styles.*[1] We all fit into at least two of these style categories. Each one has its own set of strengths and inherent messages that it conveys. Each allows you, within the broad category, to build a wardrobe aligned with your professional needs. These categories serve as a convenient template within which you can work to achieve individual

---

1 Alyce Parsons, StyleSource: The Power of the Seven Universal Styles for Women and Men, 2008.

flexibility and creativity. They enable you to choose fashions that will reflect your authentic self — within the confines of business-appropriate styles, colors and fits.

In the tables that follow, I summarize the key messages that each style communicates to the audience, as well as the design, silhouette and colors that characterize the style, along with the advantages that each offers to the wearer.

# Sporty Style

| | |
|---|---|
| **Sporty Style communicates:** | • Friendly, casual and approachable<br>• Fun, outgoing and likeable<br>• Happy and cheerful<br>• Youthful, energetic and alertness<br>• Candid, open personality<br>• Optimistic and enthusiastic<br>• Energetic and quick<br>• Unpretentious and natural |
| **Advantages** | • Brings ease and comfort into your life with relaxed, natural clothing and appearance<br>• Saves time and hassle<br>• Comfortable clothing |
| **Design** | • Classic, casual<br>• Tailored, relaxed lines<br>• Loosely structured, comfortable shape<br>• Noticeable details from active sportswear<br>• Functional, sportswear design |
| **Silhouette** | • Relaxed fit<br>• Enlarged rectangle<br>• Natural shoulders<br>• No waist or slight indentation<br>• Eased hemlines |
| **Colors** | • Neutrals: navy, tan, khaki, white<br>• Bright colors: red, blue, yellow, green<br>• Earth tones: rust, brown, gold, olive<br>• Light to medium value<br>• 3-4 colors worn in an outfit |

# Traditional Style

| Traditional Style communicates: | • Conservative and businesslike<br>• Trustworthy and loyal<br>• Authority and credibility<br>• Responsible and reliable<br>• Consistent and dependable<br>• Organized and efficient<br>• Conscientious and honest |
|---|---|
| **Advantages** | • Universally accepted business attire<br>• Classic, tailored, uniform dressing<br>• Long lasting classics, investment dressing<br>• Gives off look of being well informed and knowledgeable |
| **Design** | • Classic, timeless<br>• Tailored, straight lines<br>• Structured, permanent shape<br>• Functional design |
| **Silhouette** | • Formed shoulders<br>• Box or slightly indented waist<br>• Straight legs |
| **Colors** | • Neutrals: navy, grey, all shades of beige<br>• Deep colors: blue, forest green, burgundy<br>• Muted colors: peach, slate, blue, banana<br>• Light, medium, dark values<br>• 2-3 colors worn in an outfit |

# Elegant Style

| | |
|---|---|
| **Elegant Style communicates:** | • Cultivated and polished<br>• Meticulous and discerning<br>• Reserved and restrained<br>• Serene and polished<br>• Gracious and dignified<br>• Importance and influence |
| **Advantages** | • Elevates social and professional standing<br>• Known for good taste and discernment<br>• Flawless, impeccable appearance<br>• Classic, ensemble dressing |
| **Design** | • Classic, formal<br>• Softly tailored, smooth and simple lines<br>• Semi-structured, graceful shape<br>• Minimal details<br>• Understated design |
| **Silhouette** | • Perfect fit<br>• Natural formed shoulders<br>• Slightly defined waist |
| **Colors** | • Charcoal<br>• Dust shades: slate, mauve, celadon, wheat<br>• Monochromatic, tone-on-tone<br>• Light, medium, dark tones<br>• Subtle neutrals: cream, grey, beige, taupe |

# Romantic Style

| | |
|---|---|
| **Romantic Style communicates:** | • Supportive and caring<br>• Warm and understanding<br>• Considerate and compassionate<br>• Gentle, sensitive and non-threatening<br>• Charming and gracious<br>• Peaceful and calm |
| **Advantages** | • Inspires cooperation, not competition<br>• People feel safe and open up<br>• Provides a glowing, fresh look of youth<br>• Soft colors and fabric relax nerves |
| **Design** | • Non-classic and soft<br>• Gentle curved lines<br>• Non-structured, rounded shape<br>• Many small details<br>• Intricate design |
| **Silhouette** | • Modestly covers the body<br>• Loose hourglass (for women)<br>• Soft detailed shoulders<br>• Blouse or nipped in waist<br>• Flared hem |
| **Colors** | • Neutrals: white, ecru, dusty blue, dove grey<br>• Pastels: pink, lilac, peach, light blue, pale yellow, mint green<br>• Light to medium values<br>• 1-2 colors worn, plus multi-colored prints<br>• Analogous or monochromatic colors |

# Alluring Style

| | |
|---|---|
| **Alluring Style communicates:** | • Captivating and sensuous<br>• Fascinating and exciting<br>• Enticing and seductive<br>• Seeking attention from |
| **Advantages** | • Ego booster, reaffirming femininity or masculinity<br>• Elicits a reaction<br>• Creates body awareness |
| **Design** | • Non-classic and form fitting<br>• S-curved lines<br>• Non-structured, simple line bias patterns<br>• Minimal details<br>• Simple and body contoured |
| **Silhouette** | • Body conforming<br>• Hourglass<br>• Natural shoulders<br>• Waist emphasized<br>• Tapered hemline |
| **Colors** | • Neutrals: black and white<br>• Daring: red, pink, purple, emerald, green, turquoise, metallic gold<br>• Light and dark values<br>• 1-2 colors worn, break at waist |

# Creative Style

| | |
|---|---|
| **Creative Style communicates:** | • Innovative and imaginative<br>• Unconventional and unique<br>• Spontaneous and adventuresome<br>• Free spirited and independent<br>• Ingenious and resourceful<br>• Talented and inventive |
| **Advantages** | • Novel and eclectic way of dressing<br>• Validates individuality: not bound by clothing rules, trends<br>• "Do your own thing" dressing<br>• Saves time and money with a variety of clothing resources |
| **Design** | • Non-classic and classic<br>• Straight, curved and diagonal lines<br>• Non-structured mixed with structured<br>• Menswear and feminine details mixed<br>• Elaborate or minimal details |
| **Silhouette** | • Loose fit, or loose and tight combined<br>• Exaggerated rectangle or any silhouette<br>• Usually non-defined waist<br>• Flared or straight hemline, exaggerated length |
| **Colors** | • Neutrals: black, charcoal, maroon<br>• Neon: orange, lime green, yellow<br>• Medium to dark values<br>• One to many colors worn<br>• Murky: Khaki, olive, curry, dusty, purple, teal |

# Dramatic Style

| | |
|---|---|
| **Dramatic Style communicates:** | • Confident and self-assured<br>• Assertive and bold<br>• Demanding and intense<br>• Remote and aloof<br>• Cosmopolitan and urban<br>• Leadership, ability to influence |
| **Advantages** | • Empowering clothing: "Suit of Armor"<br>• Exaggerated look attracts attention<br>• Severe style evokes respect<br>• Fashion forward, avant-garde |
| **Design** | • Non-classic, sleek<br>• Angled, straight lines<br>• Severely structured<br>• Minimal details<br>• Stark, architectural design |
| **Silhouette** | • Semi-fitted<br>• Exaggerated inverted triangle<br>• Square shoulders<br>• Slightly defined waist<br>• Pinned hemline |
| **Colors** | • Neutrals: black and white<br>• Jewel tones: red, purple, magenta, sapphire, emerald green, chrome yellow<br>• Dark and light values<br>• Bright and intense<br>• 1-2 colors worn, contrasting colors |

# General Guidelines

As professionals, we must recognize the inherent power of professional presence and understand the impression it forms in the minds of others. At all times, we must personify excellence through the image we project. It's what colleagues and clients expect of us as leaders. Regardless of the style category that best suits you, following these guidelines will help you establish a consistent professional presence.

**Business Attire:** Lean toward the "conservative" and "traditional" when choosing professional attire. When interacting with clients, dress according to the client's environment, but aim to project an appearance that is "one notch above." Invest in tailored, high-quality business suits and well-made leather shoes for situations when formal business attire is required. Also invest in smart business casual wear, including tailored slacks, skirts, shirts, blouses, polished leather shoes and appropriate accessories (e.g., belts, watches and jewelry). Plan to wear suits to presentations and C-Suite meetings unless you are told not to (even in these situations, a jacket is highly recommended).

**Grooming:** It's important to look well-groomed, whether you're wearing business-formal or business-casual clothing. Look tidy by styling and trimming your hair (including facial hair), keeping your nails clean and trimmed, and wearing clothes that are clean and pressed. Make sure your shoes and accessories are presentable.

**Extended Image:** Reinforce a professional and organized image through your surroundings and personal belongings. Come prepared to meetings with presentable notebooks, pens, folios, and other items. Keep your laptop bag, briefcase and vehicle clean and tidy. Maintain a clutter-free workspace and automobile.

## Your Wardrobe as an Investment

Your wardrobe is an investment in self-marketing. After all, wardrobe is one of many tools needed to project professional presence, and what is professional presence if not a marketing tool? Your visual image is part of an ongoing branding campaign designed to advance your career, increase your income and enhance your professional status. As you climb the pay and status ladder, your wardrobe should reflect each new "status rung" that you reach.

I'm not suggesting that entry-level employees should max out their credit cards purchasing custom-tailored clothing, but by the time they become managers and directors, they should already be wearing clothes appropriate for managerial positions. In fact, it's less likely that people will be promoted to management if they haven't been dressing the part *in advance* of the promotion.

You can also think of your wardrobe like a house. You buy a house, and you invest in upgrading and maintaining that house. If you invest wisely in the maintenance and upgrades, you'll eventually command a higher price for the property than what you paid. If you neglect the house's appearance and infrastructure, you'll have a hard time selling it. Notice that I said "appearance" as well as infrastructure? You don't buy a $5 million home and then furnish it with items from IKEA. As an undergraduate, you can get away with that, but at some point (probably in your early thirties) your taste will be considered immature — or just plain bad — if you don't invest in higher-quality furnishings. Conversely, if you're still living in your first rental apartment by the time you reach your thirties, and you're stuffing it with pricey antiques made by 18th century Newport cabinetmakers, you're overdue for a new house or condo.

Nobody expects an entry-level employee or mid-level manager to spend a fortune on shirts, skirts, suits and ties from the likes of Barneys, Nordstrom and Nieman Marcus. As long as your clothing fits properly, accentuating strengths and camouflaging weaknesses, it's okay to buy your wardrobe off-the-rack.

The idea is to align your wardrobe with your status and income, not to dress above your station or beneath it. Your wardrobe should increase (or at least appear to increase) in value as your experience, status and income increase. Not long ago, I consulted with a manager who had "missed this memo." She had begun shopping at Express eight years before, and had never graduated from it. Here was a manager earning a mid-six-figure salary, still shopping at a store that caters to support staff and entry-level workers. (For those of you unfamiliar with Express, its offerings are similar to those found at The Gap. It offers basic clothing of so-so quality. It's fine if you're looking for polo shirts and chinos, but you won't find executive-level apparel there.)

In theory, keeping your wardrobe aligned with your image provides higher and higher returns on the investment. You make strategic wardrobe purchases, and people notice. You'll get the job because your wardrobe enhances your image or, at a minimum, doesn't *conflict* with your image. By making strategic investments, you'll repeat benefits in the form of job offers, promotions, salary raises and key assignments.

By the way, when I talk about maintaining your wardrobe, I'm referring to more than just following the care and cleaning instructions — e.g., taking dry-clean-only garments to the dry cleaners instead of tossing them into a washing machine. That's part of the maintenance equation, but only part. Even more important is ensuring that your older clothing remains a good fit — literally *a good fit.*

Choosing poorly fitting clothes is one of the most common (and glaring) mistakes that people make when they shop. As masters of our own image, it is critical that we recognize and accept a simple fact that Zen Masters constantly drill into every student: *nothing in this world is permanent, including our bodies.*

As people age, some gain weight and others lose weight. Rounded posteriors may flatten; thighs may grow plumper or leaner. In addition, blonde hair tends to darken and, eventually, everyone's hair will probably turn white or gray. Part of maintaining your wardrobe is making constant adjustments to accommodate an expanding or receding waistline, shoulders, neck, butts, or arms.

*Recognize and accept that your body will change as you grow older,* and respond to this by choosing new sizes, new styles and new colors to complement and compliment your evolving body.

Denial is not an appropriate strategy to the aging process. Such a strategy is more likely to make you a laughingstock than it is to recapture "lost youth." Maintenance is about ensuring that what you have remains appropriate. Maintenance is about selecting new clothes that are appropriate for the "physical you" that you are *today.*

I confront denial on a routine basis. Clients have gained or lost weight, but continue to wear the same clothes — the same styles, same sizes, same silhouettes and same colors. If people would just look in the mirror and see themselves as others see them (or consult a blunt-speaking friend), they would probably say, "This suit looks ridiculous! I've lost fifty pounds over the last two years, and I'm still wearing an extra-large shirt with a sixteen-inch neck. I look like a kid wearing his daddy's 'big boy' suit."

It's been nearly one hundred years since adolescents wore quasi-uniforms signaling their status as "not quite adult" (e.g., knickerbockers for boys), but the notion of age-appropriate clothing hasn't entirely vanished — nor should it.

With few exceptions, a sixty-year-old woman should not wear the same styles that she did at age eighteen — unless she wants to look like someone dressing up for Halloween. Every so often, I see fifty- and sixty-something women dressed like yesterday's teenagers. In almost every case, my first and only reaction is to shake my head and think *Another sad case of denial.*

Of course, definitions of "age-appropriate" are somewhat flexible. If you're an eighty-year-old who's often mistaken for a college student, you might get away with dressing like a high school senior rather than a senior citizen. There are exceptions to every rule. Some fifty-year-olds can pull off outfits designed for twenty-year-olds.

I once worked with a woman who said, "If you're a woman over forty, your skirt should come to the knee, not above it." I disagree. If you're older than forty and you look like Jennifer Lopez, dare to break the rules! It just so happened that this woman was assisting me with a client, and I responded, "My client looks younger than forty and looks great wearing a size 4. I'm not going to insist that she wear long skirts every day."

If you've managed to retain your youthful face and figure well into middle age, then flaunt it — within the confines, of course, of what is considered professional dress.

## Business Casual Is NOT Leisure Wear

"Business Casual" is supposed to describe dress standards that emphasize greater comfort and individuality. Business casual lets employees shed their suits and ties in favor of slacks or skirts, with collared long-sleeved shirts and blouses.

Over the last two decades, many companies have relaxed their dress standards (if only on "Casual Fridays") so workers can wear more comfortable clothing. Unfortunately, many companies fail to draw the line between attire that is appropriate for the workplace and attire that is not, causing many employees to send inconsistent messages about their organizations' brands and standards.

As a manager, you must establish a clear boundary between clothing that is "casual" and clothing that is designed for one's personal life — i.e., leisure wear. At the very least, your employees should dress a notch above the customers and clients when meeting with them in person.

---

Victoria's Secret once sold body-hugging spandex tube tops as workplace wear. Anne Fisher of *Fortune* magazine's "Ask Annie" career advice column says, "As a rule, people should avoid wearing anything that shows so much skin that it distracts other people from their work." How about body piercing, tattoos, orange hair (or other colors not found in nature), three-day stubble, no socks, micro-mini-skirts or flip-flops? In some cases, you will be guided by company policy. At Ford Motor Company, for example, "non-offensive" tattoos are permitted and body piercing is acceptable if it does not pose safety risks. Subway Restaurants permit "discreet" tattoos, but body piercing is limited to one piercing per ear. Of course, some dress code violations fall into the "unwritten" category. Typically, if you wear a nose ring to work, you may be sending the wrong message to the person responsible for your next promotion.

As a rule of thumb, business casual clothing should be clean and neat, and it should fit well. Use common sense when establishing these guidelines and enforcing them. If the image your employees project will rob them (and the company) of customers' respect, it's better to have them overdress for the environment, the occasion or the audience. Remember, you and your organization get just one chance to make a first impression. When it comes to projecting professional presence through physical appearance, the key is to be yourself *within the confines of common sense and societal conventions*. "If it feels good, do it" is not a sound philosophy for projecting a professional presence.

## Cultural Considerations

There may be instances when organizations will have to broaden their definitions of acceptable versus unacceptable dress and grooming to avoid offending — or even discriminating against — employees from certain ethnic, religious or cultural backgrounds. For example, though it makes sense for a financial services company to forbid beards, tattoos and body piercings among employees, the firm will probably have to make exceptions for personnel from the Indian subcontinent (even second-generation immigrants), because Indian women often wear nose studs, and some men are required to wear beards and/or turbans.

If there is *any* doubt on whether or not to apply the organization's dress code to a particular person or group, *consult with your human resources department first.*

On the one hand, you don't want to run afoul of any federal or state non-discrimination laws or regulations. On the other hand, if you break the rules for anyone who claims a cultural or religious exemption, it may become impossible to enforce even the most minimal dress standards for others.

# Assessment Exercise

1. What's your style? Elegant? Dramatic? Romantic?

2. How is it different at work and at play? In which style are you most comfortable?

3. How has your style changed over the years? What were you wearing ten years ago? Twenty years ago?

4. How have you adapted your clothing to the changes in your body over the last ten years?

5. Is your hairstyle the same now as it was ten years ago? Is it really still working for you, or might it be time for a change?

6. Do you receive compliments on your clothing or your hair? If not, what might you change about your appearance?

# Communication Style

## CHAPTER SIX

In a recent study conducted at Pennsylvania State University by Dr. Carla R. Chamberlin[1], it was discovered that positive non-verbal behavior increases a supervisor's perceived likability and warmth. These behaviors include:

- Physical closeness (not too distant);

- Direct body and facial orientation (facing the other person);

- Generous eye contact;

- Smiling;

- Head nods (to acknowledge and encourage others while listening);

- Animated gestures.

---

1    Chamberlin, Carla R., "Nonverbal behaviors and initial impressions of trustworthiness in teacher-supervisor relationships," Communication Education, 49, 4 (2000): 352-64.

---

Because the actual content of our speech and writing communicates just a tiny fraction of everything there is to know about us, the person who wishes to project professional presence must recognize the importance of non-verbal cues to maintain a consistent image and to avoid sending contradictory messages. No matter how well *your* words communicate confidence, competence and empathy, the image received by the listener will be inconsistent if your posture, movements, gestures, facial expressions, vocal dynamics and physical distance (proxemics) contradict what you are saying.

A luncheon speaker may glide onto the stage with the grace of a movie star, but if her voice quivers during her presentation, the audience will be painfully aware that she lacks confidence as a public speaker. A job candidate may present a résumé worthy of Leonardo DaVinci, but if his hands are pasted to his lap throughout the interview, you will quickly notice this odd behavior and wonder about its causes. You may not be conscious of the disconnect between what's being said and what's being communicated through non-verbal behavior, but you *will* detect it. And more often than not, you'll respond negatively to the person who displays unconventional and/or inappropriate behavior.

## Proxemics

Essentially, proxemics is the study of personal and private space.

One of the best illustrations of proxemics and its importance to social interactions is featured in the *Seinfeld* episode titled "The Raincoats." In this episode, Elaine introduces a new boyfriend, played by Judge Reinhold, to the gang. Jerry immediately dubs the boyfriend "a close-talker" because he stands disturbingly close to anyone he talks with, invading the individual's personal space.

We humans instinctively protect our physical bodies and our psychological welfare by erecting invisible zones around our bodies. Just as animals mark their territory with urine and other signs to establish privacy or dominance, people use furniture, fences and even wedding rings to satisfy the same needs. Our need for territorial control and ownership is ubiquitous — we have our favorite chair at home and our favorite table at the restaurant, and when we're in church, we usually sit in the same pew and show annoyance if someone else dares to sit in our place.

"It is as if we have an 'ego bubble' that surrounds each one of us and you enter another's bubble at your peril. Powerful people have a larger bubble than the rest of us — it is important to understand that one's personal distance (or proxemics) can have a direct effect on moderating what is not being said non-verbally. Interpersonal distance communicates acceptance, encouragement or rejection. Put simply — if you like or want to support someone you will move toward them; if you don't, you won't!"[2]

According to research conducted by E.T. Hall[3] more than fifty years ago, there are four major zones to recognize:

- **The Intimate Zone** (15-45 centimeters). Sometimes called the "kissing zone," this area is usually reserved for spouses, significant others and close family members. Someone in the intimate zone is literally close enough to touch you;

2　Eggert, Max A, "Body Language for Business."
3　Hall, E.T. (1966), "The Hidden Dimensions of Man's Use of Space in Public and Private."

- **The Personal Zone** (46 centimeters — 1.3 meters). In this area, touch is possible but only to parts of the body that are socially acceptable in most Western cultures — the hands, arms and shoulders. Friends and close associates are welcome in this zone. It's important to establish eye contact in this zone;

- **The Social Zone** (1.3-3.5 meters). Co-workers and customers should maintain relations in this zone. Eye contact is important in this zone, too, and voices will probably be raised above the volume needed in closer zones to maintain an air of formality;

- **The Public Zone** (more than 3.6 meters). This is the zone in which we prefer to keep strangers, as well as people we don't especially like.

Most of us are aware that someone's personal space should not be entered without permission. Invading someone's space without consent produces the "fight or flight" response (and in a business setting, it's usually the flight response). In an amusing episode of the History Channel program *United Stats of America*, hosts Randy and Jason Sklar put Hall's proxemics zones to the test by randomly trying to enter the social, personal and intimate spaces of strangers they encounter in New York's Central Park. Without fail, the "victims" responded — at first — by trying to increase the distance between themselves and the invader, finally fleeing the area when it became obvious that the experimenter had no intention of backing away.

The lesson here is obvious. On most occasions and in most environments, the person with professional presence stays in the social zones of colleagues, customers, subordinates and superiors, entering the personal zone only when he is invited or after becoming friendly with the person. There are plenty of situations in which you'll find yourself shoved into others' personal zones — elevators, airplanes, trains, etc. — but in these cases, we maintain our sense of psychological separation by averting our eyes.

## Posture

The way you stand, the way you sit, and the way you walk influence the image you project. They can convey confidence and poise, or anxiety and low self-confidence, or any combination of mixed messages. Not long ago, I watched a televised interview with a young singer who responded to the host's questions in a voice that was controlled and confident. There was just one problem. Throughout the exchange, the interviewee's face was pointed directly at the floor in front of him. He never once looked up to make eye contact with the interviewer. One could interpret the singer's posture in different ways, but none of the conclusions would be positive. At the very least, the young man was probably so nervous that he didn't want to catch a glimpse of the host, the audience or the cameramen for fear of reminding himself the interview was being taped for television — that he was being watched by hundreds of live human beings and (soon) millions more at home.

By contrast, consider the posture adopted by experienced interviewees on talk shows such as *Late Night with David Letterman* or *The Tonight Show*. The small of the guest's back rests against the back of the chair. The upper body leans slightly forward, expressing engagement with the host and the questions. The interviewee's legs are crossed at the knee, one foot planted firmly on the floor or (in the case of female guests) tucked to one side. The hands rest on the thighs (or on the table separating the guest from the host), so the interviewee can gesture naturally.

When standing, the person with professional presence is tall and erect, with shoulders back, so the chest is clearly visible instead of appearing sunken or withdrawn. The legs are aligned with the feet at hip-wide distance to ensure good balance and project confidence or even strength, and the arms are kept to the side as naturally as possible.

By following these simple guidelines, you will project an air of calm and confidence, rather than nervousness and self-consciousness. Through your posture, you want to communicate that you are alert but relaxed; engaged but not nervous; energized but not hyperactive. You want to project an image that reflects your authentic self when that authentic self is open, honest, curious and fully prepared to talk.

## Movement

Your goal with body movement is to act and react naturally — *and appropriately* — to what is said and done in the situation. When people move their bodies naturally in response to various stimuli, we pay little attention to the movements. We expect people to lean forward to express interest in what we're saying; to make eye contact with us (but not stare) when we are speaking with them; and to smile when we say something that's meant to be funny — even if it's not funny. It's only when people do *not* move in ways considered "normal" that we take notice.

For this reason, unnatural movement is a stock in trade of physical comedy. We laugh at the sitcom character who sits motionless at the breakfast table while the house literally collapses around him. We are surprised and amused at the person who explodes out of his chair, arms flailing, in response to a seemingly inoffensive comment. We empathize with the annoyance revealed in somebody's facial expression as she watches another person tap a pencil on the desktop at 300 beats per minute.

In general, natural movements require that we: (1) look before we move — i.e., observe before we react, and (2) employ a variety of movements.

## Gestures

Gestures communicate information about thoughts and emotions that you may not be expressing through language. In addition, they can add energy to a conversation that helps to capture and retain your audience's attention. Unless you want to appear stiff, boring or petrified with fear, *do not*:

- Hold your hands in front of your body;

- Fold your arms as if closing yourself off;

- Repeat the same gesture over and over;

- Wring your hands;

- Hold your hands behind your back;

- Keep your elbows stuck to your sides.

But *do*:

- Use all your arm space available for gestures;

- Turn your palms up when soliciting feedback, and turn the palms down when making a point (to show confidence).

When challenged or placed in a difficult situation, most people unknowingly cross their arms and step backward. Instead, step forward slightly and avoid crossing your arms.

Be aware that the messages sent by particular gestures in the U.S. can mean something entirely different in another country or culture. For example, although the "thumbs up" gesture is a sign of approval in the U.S., it means "up yours" in Australia. Bringing the thumb and index finger together to form a circle means "okay" in New York, but in Paris it means "you're a zero," and in most Mediterranean countries it's an obscene gesture. Keep this in mind when interacting with foreign clients and colleagues, and when you travel abroad. When in doubt, it is better to risk appearing slightly stiff and boring than to unintentionally insult the audience.

## Facial Expressions

Your facial expressions reveal your natural self. When nervous, people often overcompensate by looking serious. Don't forget to smile occasionally! Your face expresses emotion and tells the listener a lot about how you feel about your message. Facial expressions are the signals that most people rely on in their initial interactions. They provide cues by which other people interpret your mood and personality. The expression on your face can quickly trigger either a negative or positive response from the people you meet, so it's important to make positive first impressions with a pleasant and natural smile, as well as appropriate eye contact.

By the way, I don't care for the term "eye contact." I prefer to use "eye connection" because our goal is to establish a rapport with other people by meeting their eyes — just long enough to indicate that we're engaged with what they're saying. Typically, you should make an eye connection for three to six seconds. An eye connection lasting longer than six seconds is usually interpreted as *staring*.

If you want to identify the inner feelings of another person, watch the facial expressions closely. A frown may tell you something is wrong. A pleasant smile generally communicates that "things are okay." Everyone has encountered a look of surprise or a look that could kill. These facial expressions usually reflect inner emotions more accurately than words do. The smile is the most recognizable signal in the world. People everywhere tend to trust a smiling face,[4] though it can be inappropriate. Young women smiling at male strangers on the street, in some countries, is interpreted not as pleasant friendliness but as a serious come-on.

My friend Eric was introduced to the importance of facial expressions after landing his first management position. At the end of a meeting, a client asked him to complete a particular project by a deadline that Eric considered ridiculous. Although he told the client this would be "no problem" and replied that he'd probably submit the work before the deadline, the expression on his face said, "I hate your guts." Eric wasn't aware of this until his boss later pointed out the discrepancy between Eric's verbal and non-verbal communications with the client. Thereafter, Eric made a point of conducting exercises in front of a mirror, rehearsing his reactions to various types of news — pleasant and unpleasant — to ensure that his facial expressions aligned with his words. I suggest you do the same.

---

4 "Developing a Professional Presence," HM Management Space, www.college.hmco.com, June 30, 2008, p. 63

Prior to this incident, Eric had no idea that his facial expressions frequently betrayed what he was really thinking and feeling.

## Vocal Variety and Pauses

I can't think of anything more tedious than listening to someone speak in a monotone, with the exception of Ben Stein's character in *Ferris Bueller's Day Off*. (As a former economist, Stein probably had no shortage of role models for that character.) Not only is monotone speaking very boring, it also suggests that you, too, are probably a boring and lifeless individual.

Whether you're delivering a formal presentation or offering a few comments during a meeting, it's important to incorporate vocal variety. By this I mean that you should adjust the volume, the pitch, the pace and the speed of your delivery to reflect your feelings about the content. If you are passionate about a topic, your volume, pitch and inflections should reflect that passion — without making you appear hysterical. If you want to highlight a particular message, you may want to "punch" one or more sentences — i.e., speak more slowly and include dramatic pauses in order to emphasize particular words or phrases. Doing this tells the audience that you want them to pay particular attention to those words and phrases. It conveys that you have a genuine interest in the subject and want them to share the same feelings you do.

In our everyday lives, most of us do this without even thinking. When we're discussing last night's football game or an episode of our favorite TV show, we express interest and emotion by punching certain words and phrases, raising the pitch and volume of our voices and using pauses to punctuate key points. It's only when we become nervous and self-conscious that we must *remember* to do these things to avoid appearing disinterested. Even if we're not interested or excited about the material, we must *appear* to be. We don't want to look like we're merely going through the motions to fulfill a professional obligation, or that we'd rather be mowing the lawn. That detracts from professional presence.

If displaying interest and excitement (or faking it) is a problem, I suggest you take a class in public speaking, join an organization such as Toastmasters or even take an acting class or two. At a minimum, these activities will help you to become more aware of how and when to employ different speech and presentation techniques without sounding like a cheap salesman.

Speaking of cheap salesmen ...

Some people are so used to "being on" that they lose the ability to turn off their sales and marketing persona. Last year, one of my friends met with a client in a marathon information-gathering session. During the morning, the client delivered a PowerPoint presentation highlighting his company's core products and services. Afterward, my friend and the client went to lunch — and the client was unable to switch from "presentation mode" to "conversation mode." The volume of his voice remained so high and dramatic that a couple dining thirty feet away asked him to tone it down. Unfortunately, this proved impossible. He was unable to adjust from the role of presenter to the role of lunch companion. The man was like a wind-up doll that had been permanently set to the "sell, Sell, SELL!" position.

By the way, pausing also offers you an opportunity to:

- Breathe;

- Think;

- Eliminate language clutter such as um, uh, like, you know;

- Eliminate over-used words such as basically, actually, okay;

- Eliminate mouth noises — e.g., the soft "tk" sounds produced when you separate your tongue from the roof of your mouth. (In normal conversation, these noises are barely audible, but when amplified by a microphone, they can sound like action-movie sound effects.);

- Appear more confident by demonstrating that you are comfortable with short periods of silence — as opposed to the person who is so afraid of "awkward" pauses that she would rather keep blabbing until the audience can no longer stand the sound of her voice;

- Allow the audience to reflect on what you just said;

- Add emphasis to the previous statement;

- Encourage others to speak — e.g., during a Q&A session.

# The Handshake

Although you've shaken hands with hundreds or thousands of people, you probably have no idea whether your handshake makes a positive or negative first impression. For that reason, it's a good idea to have your image consultant (or trusted friends and colleagues) provide you with an honest evaluation of your handshake.

A handshake should communicate warmth and genuine concern for others. It should convey strength, but not brutality — watch out for women with small hands and several rings, because a killer grip will really hurt their hand. A handshake should convey confidence but not arrogance. Above all, your handshake should not communicate weakness or nervousness — a friend once told me his boss's handshake was like handing someone a dead fish. The message you send through the handshake is conveyed through a combination of the following five factors:

- **Firmness:** In general, a firm — but not a knuckle-crushing — handshake communicates a caring attitude. On the other hand, a weak grip conveys indifference or aloofness;

- **Dry versus sweaty palms:** A sweaty palm not only produces an "ick" factor in the other person, but also communicates that you are nervous. If moist palms are frequently a problem, carry a handkerchief, and discreetly wipe your hand just before you shake someone's hand;

- **Duration:** There is no rule for how long a good handshake should last — only that it shouldn't be so short that you give the impression that you'd rather not shake the other person's hand, nor so long that he will expect you to drop to one knee and produce an engagement ring. Pay attention to the other person's handshake, and quit when they're ready;

- **Depth:** A full, deep grip is more likely to convey friendship. Position your hand to make complete contact with the other person's hand and, once you've connected, close your thumb over the back of the other person's hand and give a slight squeeze;

- **Eye Connection:** Visual contact will increase the positive message sent by your handshake. Make a quick connection, but don't stare.[5]

Recognizing the key components of positive non-verbal communication will help you bolster internal confidence and calm. This is something that has long been known to professional actors. They are taught that one way to "get into character" is by adopting the non-verbal habits of that character. This is known as the "outward-in approach." If you want to look like someone who is confident and self-assured, start by projecting the *outward* appearance of someone who's confident and self-assured. In the beginning, you will be merely acting the part of someone with executive presence, but eventually these attributes will be internalized, and you will *become* a person with executive presence.

Zen Masters do something similar. They have students use a specific posture when performing the sitting meditation of "zazen." The reasoning is that function will eventually follow

---

5   "Developing a Professional Presence," HM Management Space, p. 65

form. In other words, by adopting a comfortable and stable posture that is conducive for quiet contemplation, the students will eventually train themselves to *enter* that state of quiet contemplation under almost any circumstances.

One of my colleagues applies Zen principles to golf. Instead of trying to visualize the path of the ball that he's about to strike with a club, he focuses on the form of his golf swing. As long as he chooses the correct club and follows the proper form for the swing, he knows that he will achieve his goal — i.e., the ball will travel the proper distance and in the right direction.

The same is true of professional presence. If you employ the techniques of professional presence, you will project professional presence from the get-go.

## General Guidelines

Whenever we place a phone call, send an e-mail or conduct a face-to-face meeting, we have an opportunity to reinforce our professional presence. As you interact with clients and colleagues, be mindful of the perceptions they may form based on how you communicate. In general, make it a point to adhere to the following standards:

**Oral Communication:** Speak clearly and concisely, using appropriate language and tone. Speak in a way that is courteous and respectful to everyone you interact with, not just the clients. Minimize your use of consulting, business or industry jargon, as well as colloquialisms. Avoid slang and profanity that others might find offensive. Adjust your style, tone, pitch, pace and volume based on your audience.

**Written Communication:** Make sure that you demonstrate professionalism in all of your written communications by leaning toward the formal. Include a salutation and signature in your messages to demonstrate a high level of respect and courtesy. Use proper punctuation, grammar, and capitalization in all forms of communication, even instant messages and text messages. Apply best-practice guidelines to your writing style (e.g., *Elements of Style* by Strunk & White, *Minto Pyramid Principle* by Barbara Minto).

**Non-Verbal Communication:** Always be aware of your body language, facial expressions, eye connections and hand gestures. Doing so will instantly help you become a better communicator.

# Assessment Exercise

1. Think about your handshake. What do you think it conveys? Is it professional? How does it compare with the handshake of a person you trust?

2. Shake hands with a trusted friend or colleague and then ask them about your handshake.

3. Watch others closely for a couple of days and assess their "physical closeness" to others. Can you spot people who are too close? Can you see others backing away from that closeness?

4. Stand before a mirror and pretend a client has just asked you about a ridiculous deadline. Try two responses — one response indicating you can meet that deadline and another explaining why you can't. Gauge the look on your face (and your other body language) to assess your honesty and professionalism with each response.

5. Pay attention for several days to the "eye connections" you make with others, and what you see others doing with you. Can you recognize eye connections that are too long or short? Too often or not often enough? Note your own reactions to the eye connections you get from others.

# Business Etiquette

## CHAPTER SEVEN

**M**y friend George learned most of what he knows about business etiquette the hard way — through unexpected trials and embarrassing errors. Back in the early '90s, when he was editorial director of a New York PR firm, part of his job was conducting media and message training seminars, along with the head of the agency.

On one occasion, he had just finished a marathon workshop with the executives of a high-tech company headquartered in La Jolla, California. He was "tired as all hell" and just wanted to go home. After packing up their video cameras, lights and other gear, George and his boss were escorted to a waiting taxi by the company's sixty-something CEO. En route, the man offered to help George carry some of the cases he was lugging toward the curb.

Without thinking, George handed the man almost everything he had been carrying and hurried toward the taxi. George's boss took the heavy equipment from the older gentleman to prevent "an incident" — e.g., heart attack or stroke — and once they were inside the car, he gave George a tongue-lashing over the *faux pas*. George was told that he had violated business etiquette by treating the client like a pack mule. "He was just being polite, you dunce! You were supposed to hand him your briefcase, not a hundred pounds of video equipment."

He was right. That was *not* good business etiquette.

In part, George's mistake was caused by his own exhaustion. However, he also admitted that he had never received any schooling in business etiquette. Instead, he had learned most of what he knew from watching old movies. This explains why he thought it was acceptable to drink three martinis at a client luncheon — like Cary Grant in *North by Northwest* (1959).

Following proper business etiquette requires that you (a) actually know how to behave in every situation that you're likely to encounter as a professional; and (b) that you actually *follow* these rules, regardless of any temptations to the contrary.

Keep in mind that social and business etiquette varies from company to company, and among nations, religions, cultures and social identity groups. Also, be aware that business is becoming increasingly diverse. On the one hand, therefore, we must respect and accommodate different cultures. On the other hand, we don't have to succumb to silly (and sometimes insulting) political correctness.

Also known as manners and protocol, etiquette is a set of traditions designed to promote politeness, kindness and efficiency. Following the appropriate behavioral guidelines for the environment, audience, occasion — and your assigned role — means you will never have to worry about sending the wrong message or embarrassing yourself. Without having to be conscious of it, you will automatically display consideration, civility and kindness toward others, as long as you observe proper etiquette. You will never needlessly offend others by accidentally violating social conventions and taboos.

In short, observing proper business and social etiquette demonstrates that you genuinely care about other people and not just yourself.

The specifics of etiquette depend on the environment, the occasion, the audience, and your role. This is why we have one set of rules for behavior in the office and another for entertaining clients over meals.

In today's competitive marketplace, every business interaction is a brand-building opportunity. Regardless of corporate branding efforts, your clients experience your company through the teams and people who work side-by-side with them. These experiences take place over meals, in the boardroom and at social gatherings. It is up to *you* to deliver the highest level of integrity and professionalism — deliverables that will build your company's brand and your own reputation.

Because this is not a book of etiquette, I won't offer an exhaustive list of rules and guidelines for every occasion. In general, just be aware of the following:

**Office Etiquette:** Be respectful and courteous to others in the workplace in all business settings. Be aware of your personal noise level (e.g., cell phones, voice volume) in small or open work spaces. If you work in a client-serving capacity, as I did for many years, maintain a clean and tidy workspace, especially at the client's site and in office hoteling environments. Avoid activities that could be negatively perceived by clients

(e.g., listening to an iPod, cellphone calls, checking Facebook or email.)

**Social Etiquette:** Uphold a level of professional conduct and behavior in all social settings, no matter how fun or jovial the atmosphere. Avoid too much alcohol, which can result in embarrassment for you, your team or the client. Know and practice essential table manners when dining for business — or after business. Understand the expectations of your role as the host or guest at an event.

**Public Etiquette:** Maintain high standards of professional conduct and behavior in public, regardless of whether you're on company or personal time. Avoid speaking about clients or colleagues in a manner that could be perceived negatively. Avoid discussing confidential internal or client information in public places (e.g., airports, taxis, restaurants, lounges). Be mindful of what you communicate using social media because clients and colleagues are often linked to your networks. Use laptop privacy screens when working in public places.

When it comes to etiquette, the biggest problem confronting the average professional is ignorance — sheer ignorance. A surprising number of businesspeople are not only unaware of the correct etiquette for a client dinner or for cell phone use; they also aren't aware that there even is etiquette for these activities. It's hardly surprising then that many businesspeople don't behave appropriately. They don't know how to behave appropriately because nobody ever told them what to do and what to avoid.

Unfortunately, good manners and comportment are not taught in most schools. It is something that parents are expected to teach their children, based on the assumption that the parents were actually taught these rules. This may come as a shock, but many parents know less about etiquette than their children do. Some business owners and senior managers know less about etiquette than their employees do. It is a case of the blind leading the blind or, more accurately, a case of the blind letting the blind stumble into concrete abutments.

Do not follow the path taken by my friend George. Do not wait until you get chewed out by the boss or, worse, until you lose a prospective client because you didn't know it was impolite to take cell phone calls during the sales meeting or because you stole his roll at dinner.

Learn the rules, and follow them.

Learn them, live them, and learn to love them. They will spare you from many an embarrassing and career-crushing debacle.

Always remember: rules of etiquette are not in place to enforce mindless conformity. *They serve to bolster civility.* They demonstrate that you are a knowledgeable, cultured, considerate and caring person, not an egomaniac who thinks he is the center of the universe. If you genuinely believe that the sun revolves around your head, then there is nothing that I or any image consultant can do. You are too important to read this book, too important to stop texting friends during a meeting, and too important to keep from making tasteless jokes at funerals.

## Etiquette Is Not Political Correctness

If ignorance is the biggest etiquette problem I confront, the second biggest problem is people who do not know the difference between etiquette and political correctness (PC). They are *not* the same thing.

Political correctness is a category of speech and behavior specifically designed to avoid giving offense to a social identity group (SIG), whether that identity is based on ethnicity, religion, sexual-orientation, or some other factor. My problem with political correctness lies not with its desire to treat people with civility and respect — these are laudable goals. In fact, these are two of the same goals underlying the basic rules of etiquette. My problem with political correctness is that most of its practitioners have a tendency to:

- Disregard well-established rules of civility in favor of whatever "flavor of the month" is atop the PC menu;

- Proselytize rules based on the conventional wisdom that prevails in their own political, socio-economic and cultural "opinion bubbles." In short, they demand that speech and conduct developed by and for their own SIG be mimicked by everyone else;

- Ignore the fact that every SIG comprises a variety of individuals with diverse opinions, beliefs, sensitivities, etc.

For example, in my travels I have met "Native Americans" who hail from many regions and ancestries. Some insist on being identified as "Native American." Others loathe the term, and prefer "American Indian" or just "Indian." Others would rather be identified by their tribe — or not identified by ethnicity at all. By insisting that everyone refer to (say) members of the Cherokee tribe as "Native Americans" regardless of the wishes of the individuals in the tribe, the politically correct impose their preferences on other people. *That* is not the point of etiquette. Etiquette is not about you and your preferences and tastes. It is about other people — about treating everyone with uniform respect and courtesy *according to rules dictated by the occasion, the environment and the company — not the rules that you and your SIG have invented.*

If you observe the right etiquette for the occasion, the environment, the audience, and your role (and exercise some common sense), you are almost guaranteed to avoid offending others. That is one of the main purposes of etiquette — to ensure that everyone behaves properly without having to review (in advance) a psychological profile of everyone in the room. I said "almost guaranteed" because, every so often, you'll encounter someone who seems to enjoy taking offense — someone who seeks any excuse to manufacture self-righteous outrage. These people will take offense at the drop of a pin because they have a chip on their shoulder and are looking for the opportunity to take offense. In these cases, there is little you can do but flee from their company at the earliest convenient moment. It is not your place to refer them to an anger-management specialist, though they could probably benefit from one.

Remember, etiquette is designed for everyone's benefit.

Memorizing a few simple do's and don'ts won't tarnish your spontaneity, effervescence or quirky sense of humor. You can display these amazing personality traits without displaying a lack of etiquette.

Knowing which fork to use, where your bread plate is, where your water glass is, and how to pass food items at dinner has *nothing* to do with being politically correct. Etiquette is about being appropriate. It is about showing that you are cultured, educated and aware.

As a professional, it is critical that you demonstrate awareness of which behavior is correct and which is not.

Being politically correct is different. Being politically correct requires that you make assumptions about others based on preconceptions.

# When in Doubt, Ask

You will never have to worry about political correctness again if you *ask questions and actively listen to the responses.*

Before choosing a restaurant at which to meet your new clients, ask about their preferences. Don't assume that the clients from Memphis are interested only in barbecued ribs and collard greens. For all you know, they may be vegetarians who grew up in Berkeley. Or maybe they're so accustomed to the style of barbecue served in their hometown that they'll recoil from the Memphis, Kansas City or Texas style.

If you are not sure how to address someone new, ask whether she prefers to be called by her first name or as Ms. or Mrs. or even Doctor (if she has a PhD). These days, most people are comfortable being addressed by their first names, but there are always exceptions. When in doubt, ask.

A few years ago, I was traveling in Asia when a member of my group referred to Asian people as Orientals. Initially, I was taken aback, since that term has long been politically incorrect in the U.S. However, I soon learned from this colleague (who is of Oriental/Asian descent) that the word is both acceptable and widely used throughout much of Asia.

*Do not assume that American standards are universal.* When meeting someone from a different country or culture, take a moment to ask, "What do you prefer to be called?" or "How would you like us to refer to your countrymen?" or "What's the appropriate terminology for _____?"

*That's good etiquette.* It demonstrates awareness and humility, provided you broach the topic with some sensitivity. Obviously, it's also possible to ask such questions in a condescending or disrespectful way. It is one thing to ask a group of Japanese businessmen, "What is the appropriate terminology for a Japanese businessman in Japan?" and it is quite another to ask, "What do you people like to be called — Asians, Orientals, or Japanese?" The latter comes across as disrespectful because the underlying tone is perfunctory. It suggests that your real attitude is "I don't give a crap about addressing you with respect and courtesy, but my company takes a dim view of insulting foreigners. Whatever."

Use some discretion and common sense when learning what is appropriate.

Be informed.

Be aware.

If possible, do some homework *before* meeting with colleagues or clients from different countries and cultures. At the very least, learn what not to say or do. (Perform a quick Internet search for a list of major Don'ts that apply to that culture — like giving an Australian the "thumbs up" or using the word "fanny" when traveling Down Under.)

Do not make the classic TV sitcom mistake of memorizing a few words or phrases in the client's native language without first consulting a native speaker to learn if these words and phrases actually mean what you think they mean. On television, hilarity ensues from garbled translations. In real life, quiet embarrassment is the usual result. Businesspeople are more likely to look like idiots by showing off "knowledge" gleaned from Google Translate.

Finally, please note that pointing out another person's *faux pas* is a *faux pas* in itself. George's boss waited until they were alone in the taxi before chastising him for his rude treatment of the client. He did not humiliate him in front of the CEO. If a colleague or client makes a mistake during a meeting or over dinner, it is better to change the subject than to allow an awkward silence to envelop everyone or, worse, to point out the person's mistake.

Take a cue from the famous (and possibly apocryphal) story of the state dinner hosted by Queen Victoria. At the beginning of the legendary meal, a foreign dignitary was alleged to have used his fingerbowl as a water glass, sipping the contents of a vessel meant for washing fingers. Rather than embarrass the dignitary, Victoria made a point of drinking from *her* fingerbowl to avoid embarrassing the man — and the other dinner guests followed suit.

By the way, whenever you are entertaining clients at a restaurant, it is always a good idea to avoid foods that are likely to end up on your clothing — e.g., mussels with marinara or seafood dunked in a white wine garlic sauce. And regardless of how formal or informal the occasion, keep your alcohol consumption moderate. Many, *many* journeys to catastrophe begin when somebody gets sloppy drunk at an office party or a client dinner. In the movie *Gladiator*, Maximus said, "What we do in life echoes in eternity." By the same token, what we do at the office Christmas party can echo throughout the rest of our career with the company — and sometimes beyond.

# Managing Stereotypes

Like it or not, we cannot control every facet of our image. Some components are bequeathed by our parents and the circumstances into which we were born, including height, body shape, gender, race, ethnicity, regional accent and sexual orientation, and (to a greater or lesser degree) our spiritual views, ethics and morals. These are the foundations of the social identity groups (SIGs) to which we belong, and most of us belong to more than one SIG.

Like it or not, there are stereotypes and caricatures (positive and negative) associated with every SIG. These labels were created and reinforced by competing SIGs and the popular culture at one time or another.

Regardless of whether a stereotype is trendy and PC or antiquated and racist, it's important to recognize that it exists. If a stereotype associated with one of your SIGs is negative, you may never meet another professional who will admit to knowing about the negative stereotype. In my experience, however, it's likely that the person *is* aware of the stereotype and may even use it to evaluate people in that SIG. Even if the person believes that stereotyping is bad, and he does his best to force these views out of his brain, he may not succeed, thanks to a lifetime of conditioning.

For example, if your boss's experiences, upbringing and/or exposure to popular culture has taught him to think that Asians are good at math, but lousy drivers, his first impressions of Asians and Asian-Americans will probably be influenced, if only subconsciously, by this long-term external conditioning — no matter how hard he consciously tries to avoid making judgments based on the cliché.

At one level or another, stereotypes affect how we perceive the personal and professional images of others. Because of this, the odds are high that you will be treated better or worse than you deserve at some point in your career, thanks to a positive or negative stereotype associated with your SIG — or your *perceived* SIG. (It's not uncommon for people to mistakenly assume that someone belongs to a certain SIG based on stereotypical "clues," which is why style-conscious, well-groomed men are sometimes mistaken for gay, or outspoken savvy women who don't exaggerate their femininity are considered likely lesbian.) In other words, at one time or another, most of us will experience significant incongruence between the image we want to project and the image that is perceived by others, thanks to stereotyping.

According to Professor Laura Morgan Roberts of Harvard Business School, this incongruence affects how others assess our technical competence, social competence, character and commitment:

> *All professionals will experience a "predicament"*
> *or event that reflects poorly on their competence,*
> *character, or commitment at some point in time,*
> *due to mistakes they have made in the past that*
> *have become public knowledge, or competency*
> *gaps (e.g., shortcomings or limitations in skill set*
> *or style).*

> *Members of negatively stereotyped identity*
> *groups may experience an additional form of*
> *identity threat known as "devaluation." Identity*
> *devaluation occurs when negative attributions*
> *about your social identity group(s) undermine*

*key constituents' perceptions of your competence, character or commitment. For example, African American men are stereotyped as being less intelligent and more likely to engage in criminal behavior than Caucasian men ... Working mothers are stereotyped as being less committed to their profession and less loyal to their employing organizations. All of these stereotypes pose obstacles for creating a positive professional image.*

*Even positive stereotypes can pose a challenge for creating a positive professional image if someone is perceived as being unable to live up to favorable expectations of their social identity group(s). For example, clients may question the qualifications of a freshly minted MBA who is representing a prominent strategic consulting firm. Similarly, female medical students and residents are often mistaken for nurses or orderlies and challenged by patients who do not believe that they are legitimate physicians.[1]*

To combat negative stereotypes and better manage one's image, Professor Roberts recommends that professionals adopt various "impression management strategies" to explain predicaments, counter devaluation, and demonstrate competence and commitment.

---

1   Mallory Stark, "Creating a Positive Professional Image," *Harvard Business School Working Knowledge*, June 20, 2005.

Brett Glirbas, an entrepreneur with cerebral palsy who uses an electric wheelchair, counters negative impressions through his impeccable dress and grooming:

"People see a wheelchair and many make immediate assumptions," he says. "They have no idea that I graduated from college with honors and have my own grant-writing and consulting business. Little do they realize that I could be — and often am — an asset to companies just like theirs. They're not doing either of us any favors by assuming that my abilities are limited because of my appearance.

"When I began my career, I began to think more about how I was dressing and presenting myself to counteract some of these negative first impressions. I came to an important realization. If I waited for everyone in the world to learn that a wheelchair doesn't mean I'm less useful, then I would have a long and lonely wait. By dressing sharp and forcing people to see me as someone in control of his own appearance (and often someone in much better control than they are), I've preempted the stereotype.

"When I am dressed well, I feel more confident and more motivated to get things done. It's a daily reminder that I define myself, not anyone else. This ends up having a tangible benefit beyond how I'm feeling. People pay attention to men who are dressed well. A lot of guys are just happy to fit in with the crowd, but I have learned that there are benefits to standing out. Being well-dressed on a daily basis means more people know your name and remember you. This comes in handy when you are seeking a promotion or just trying to get noticed by someone special."[2]

---

Professor Roberts' research suggests that people can take control of their images by adopting strategies and tactics that distinguish them as individuals and educate people about the positive qualities of their SIGs.

Rather than adopting one strategy wholesale, most people use a variety of strategies for managing impressions of their social identities. In some situations, they choose to draw attention to a social identity, if they think it will benefit them personally or professionally. Even members of devalued social identity groups, such as African American professionals, will draw attention to their race if it creates mutual understanding with colleagues, generates high-quality connections with clients, or enhances their experience of authenticity and fulfillment in their work. In other situations, these same individuals may choose to minimize their race in order to draw attention to an alternate identity — such as gender, profession or religion — if they believe their race inhibits their ability to connect with colleagues or clients.

# Authentic and Appropriate

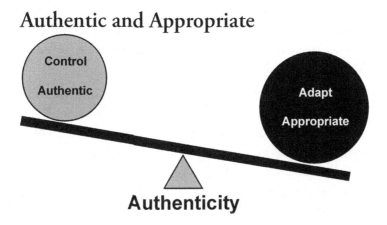

**Figure 4: Authentic and Appropriate.**

Successful impression management can generate a number of important personal and organizational benefits, including career advancement, client satisfaction, better work relationships (trust, intimacy, avoiding offense), group cohesiveness, a more pleasant organizational climate, and a more fulfilling work experience. However, when unsuccessfully used, attempts at impression management can lead to feelings of deception, delusion, preoccupation, distraction, futility and even manipulation.

If you suppress or contradict your personal values or identity characteristics for the sake of meeting societal expectations for professionalism, you might receive certain professional benefits, but you might compromise other psychological, relational and organizational outcomes.[3]

In my experience, the key to successfully projecting a professional image that counters negative stereotypes and integrates positive stereotypes is to *always* be true to your authentic self. If you don't feel comfortable emphasizing your race, ethnicity, religion or sexual orientation because it has little to do with who you are, don't try to emphasize those characteristics. There is no need to hide these traits or to be ashamed of them, but don't make a big deal of them either — that can backfire on you.

As an example, a good friend of mine years ago was in a high-level job in the federal government in Washington, D.C., and had worked with a not-really-effective employee for a little more than two years. On a particularly trying day, my friend told this employee that he really needed to go back and re-work a recently completed report because it just didn't measure up — and it had to. The employee inhaled deeply and said,

---

3    Ibid.

"You're just saying that because I'm black." My friend blinked a few times and replied, "I never noticed before that you were black, but that's what I'll see first from now on."

If projecting an image tied, in part, to your SIG feels forced and phony, chances are it will come across as forced and phony if you try to take advantage of it or draw attention to it. Ultimately, remember that *you are the author of your own image.* To take control of your image, follow Professor Roberts' advice and, as a first step, identify the ideal image you really want to project. Begin by asking yourself these questions:

- What core competencies and character traits do I want people to associate with me?

- Which of my social identities (you have more than one) do I want to emphasize and incorporate into my *workplace* interactions, and which would I rather minimize?

- What are my organization's expectations for a professional?

- How do others currently perceive me?

- Do I want to change those perceptions?

- Am I *capable* of changing my current image to match others' expectations and/or would such a change be worth the cost?

- Do I genuinely care if people have a negative perception of me?

- Which people's perception of me do I care about, and which people's perception do I not care about?

If you decide that you do want to modify your image, use strategic self-presentation to manage impressions and enhance your current image. Build your credibility while maintaining your authenticity by selecting SIG-based characteristics to emphasize — the characteristics that represent a natural fit for you and with which you feel comfortable. Then, monitor how other people react to your evolving image, along with monitoring your own behavior. Make a note of what works and what does not work and, above all, do not go overboard with the makeover campaign.

I do not want to learn that one of my readers with Arapaho ancestry showed up for work one day dressed like the Indian chief from the "The Village People" band, but if I hear about really positive co-worker feedback from a reader who finally let people know about her Nez Perce ancestry, that would be excellent.

## Active Listening

A person with executive presence is an active listener. He demonstrates that he is engaged with what others are saying and that he cares about their points of view. Through his actions, he reveals that he does not think he is the center of the universe. These are the attributes of a memorable and magnetic leader.

Most people are not active listeners. Even professionals who routinely practice public speaking or who rehearse sales pitches and conversations with customers are sometimes poor listeners. Of course, to practice active listening, you must first understand what it really means.

What distinguishes active listening from other styles of listening employed by most people?

Active listening means you are genuinely *focused* on what someone else is saying, not just pausing to be polite. It means listening not just to what someone says, but also "listening" to the person's facial expressions, posture, gestures and movements. Your goal is to absorb everything the person is communicating — verbally and non-verbally. Only by actively listening will you be able to respond appropriately and directly, which will also demonstrate that you care about the person because — well, you actually *do* care about the person.

You cannot fake active listening — not for any length of time.

What separates managers with executive presence from adequate managers is that the former actually *want* to engage in back-and-forth dialogue. They actually *want* to exchange ideas, opinions and information. They want to hear what others have to say, because gathering ideas, opinions and information from others is one of their goals. If someone with executive presence doesn't want feedback, she doesn't solicit it. When she does want to hear other points of view, she really listens to them. In short, she doesn't view every interaction as a transaction — a sale — that she will either win or lose.

Instead of focusing entirely on the results she hopes to achieve from each interaction, the person with executive presence is flexible. She is not afraid to go off-script when circumstances warrant it. Therefore, she sometimes allows her colleagues' opinions and concerns to change the direction of the meeting — or even change the original goals she brought with her to the meeting.

By contrast, the manager who is merely adequate (or worse) is so focused on achieving specific transactional results that he frequently ignores what others say. Because his goal is to push his agenda, he tends to regard different views as obstacles to be overcome, and he responds to them in the same way that telemarketers respond to the objections of prospective customers — with generic and/or rehearsed answers that may or may not have anything to do with what the other person was saying.

A veteran financial advisor, Larry enjoyed a healthy income, belonged to two country clubs, and drove a brand new 7-Series BMW. To project exactly the right image, he worked with an advertising agency to create what he now calls "a beautiful $15,000 puff piece that has cost me business."

Larry was right: his new brochure was beautiful. It described how he could provide every conceivable wealth management service, creating the expectation that he offered something very special. He couldn't wait to begin using it. However, the results were not what he anticipated. Within two weeks, Larry had lost an existing client and an affluent prospect.

Larry met with his client, presented his new brochure, and began talking about all the new services he was going to provide. His client, a business owner, peppered him with probing questions that Larry found difficult to answer. Larry's prospect also asked detailed questions prompted by the brochure, and Larry stumbled at responding to these, too. The client ended the meeting by saying that he was not confident in Larry's ability to deliver all those services, and he was going to close his account.[4]

4   Oechsli, Matt, "Becoming a Rainmaker: Creating a Downpour of Money." Overland Park, KS: Wealth Management Press, 2006

Larry learned the hard way that no matter how slick and glossy your physical image, if you don't know how to actively listen and respond to clients' concerns directly and appropriately, they will see you for what you really are — someone who is concerned only with selling something instead of helping clients solve their problems.

In my experience, salespeople make some of the best listeners — and also some of the worst. That's because every salesperson approaches customer interactions from a transactional point of view. After all, the main goal of every salesperson is to sell something to the customer.

The difference between a true "rainmaker" and the stereotypical used-car salesman is active listening. The rainmaker *listens* to his prospective customer to determine if what he is selling can actually help the person. Then the salesman works with the customer to arrive at custom solutions that will match the customer's budget, timelines, and other issues.

An adequate salesman doesn't care about the customer or his problems, so he is not inclined to actively listen. His one and only objective is to make the sale. He doesn't care if the product or service benefits the customer. He cares only about his commissions — and the savvy consumer can spot this attitude in an instant.

Last winter, a colleague — we'll call him "Bill" — learned that his home's heating and air-conditioning system was on the brink of collapse. He learned this following an inspection from a company with which he had an extended service contract. After reviewing the diagnosis, Bill scheduled an appointment with one of the company's salespeople — let's call him "Frank." Unfortunately, Frank proved to be the kind of salesman who gives the profession a bad name.

From the outset, Bill explained that because he had a limited budget, he was interested only in repairing what was broken, and not upgrading to a better system. Frank ignored the request and spent the next two hours testing Bill's patience to its limits. Frank meticulously walked Bill through one brochure after another. He touted the benefits and features of various gold- and platinum-level HVAC systems, none of which was within Bill's budget. Frank kept stressing useless "benefits" in which Bill showed *no interest* — e.g., that the company's workers were all non-smokers without prison records. (By the end of the night, Bill said he didn't care if the workers arrived in orange jumpsuits, smoking clove cigarettes, as long as they fixed everything for a reasonable price). In retrospect, said Bill, the salesman's approach seemed to be an exercise in *active non-listening* — a form of torture designed to wear down the prospect until he was willing to pay any price just to end the ordeal. At one point, Frank even pulled the old high-pressure technique of claiming that his boss would cut a few hundred dollars from the price of an expensive HVAC system if Bill committed to buying it within the next 12 hours.

Unsurprisingly, Bill purchased nothing from this salesman. In fact, he refused to return the man's calls over the next two weeks.

Instead, he bought exactly what he wanted from another company's salesman — someone who actually took time to listen. The new salesman, Al, initiated the conversation by asking Bill what he wanted and for how much. Al listened patiently, took notes, and responded to Bill's questions with concise forthright answers. He told Bill he could easily repair the damaged system with replacement units priced from A through Z. He quickly explained the benefits and features of each new unit, and again responded with specific answers to Bill's questions. The whole transaction was done in 20 minutes.

Al made the sale, and he made it look effortless. It *should* have been effortless. Bill was anxious to fix his home's HVAC system before the weather turned cold. It wasn't so much that Al was an amazing salesman; he was simply a good listener. He responded to the customer's questions and concerns. He didn't have to make an amazing sales pitch and exercise mesmerizing powers of persuasion.

Al didn't talk his way into a sale. He listened his way into a sale. Conversely, Frank talked his way out of the sale by refusing to listen.

In many meetings, attendees seem to have just one purpose in mind — to deliver their lines and leave. They seem to have no interest in what anyone else says. They don't actively listen. They don't exchange views. They don't brainstorm. They don't modify their views or even (gasp!) change their minds.

Unfortunately, some of these seemingly disinterested people *may* be listening — actively listening — without *showing* that they are listening. Someone with executive presence always shows that he is listening. And the best way to do that is to look at the person who's speaking and take notes. It is important to show the person speaking that you appreciate that he is talking. Just as you show the barista at the local Starbucks that you appreciate her service by making sure she *sees* you placing money in the tip jar, you must ensure that the speaker at a meeting sees you listening to what he is saying.

Again, this is not something you can fake — at least not consistently. If you merely point your face toward the speaker and zone out, your inattentiveness will be revealed the moment it is discovered that you have not absorbed the content.

By the way, if you want to take notes, I recommend that you ask permission at the beginning of the meeting or presentation. Otherwise, the speaker may conclude that you are texting friends/colleagues or working on another project — i.e., doing the very opposite of listening. The same behavior that can demonstrate active listening can also demonstrate preoccupation with another task unless you ask the speaker "May I take notes?" to indicate that you are recording what he is saying and not just making a grocery list.

*Tip*: When taking notes, strive to record the major points rather than creating a full transcript of the conversation like a court reporter. That way, you won't be so preoccupied with capturing every thought that you don't have time to look at the speaker.

I see examples of passive listening every day; it has become more common with each passing year. Over the last decade or so, it has become routine to walk into meetings and see a half dozen employees punching the keys of their laptops while someone is speaking. Many of them could be typing notes, but from my perspective, they may as well be checking email or playing computer games. Remember, perception is everything when it comes to professional presence. If you do not *appear* to be engaged, it may not matter that you *are* engaged. To show that you are actively listening,

DO:

- Make eye connections with the speaker;

- Ask intelligent questions — as opposed to "What was that?";

- Lean forward and look at the speaker;

- Nod your head — but don't overdo it;

- Shake your head. (This usually indicates that you disagree with what is being said, but at least it shows that you are listening.)

DO NOT:

- Text or otherwise use your cell phone. If you absolutely must make or take a call, quietly excuse yourself from the room and find a private area to conduct the conversation;

- Type on your laptop or mobile device unless you have been designated as a note-taker or have asked permission;

- Multitask by checking email or proofreading documents or anything else on your laptop;

- Distract the speaker by fidgeting in your seat, tapping a pen on the table, repeatedly coughing or clearing your throat, or otherwise hinting that you are bored or anxious.

Active listening ties in to executive presence because it shows that you are engaged, empathetic and genuine. It shows that you are genuinely interested in what the person is saying. If I'm looking past you while you are talking, or checking my email or fidgeting with papers, it suggests I really do not care about you and what you have to say. I'm focused on *myself* and not you.

I cannot think of a better example of a "professional" who personifies the very antithesis of the active listener than the CEO mentioned in a recent article by Robert I. Sutton, PhD, author of the *New York Times* bestseller *Good Boss, Bad Boss*:

*I ran a workshop for the top 50 or so executives of a large and profitable firm. Their ability to "fight as if they were right and to listen as if they were wrong" was exemplary for the first 30 minutes or so — until the CEO walked in (everyone else had been on time).*

*The CEO laughed loudly at the studies I cited and the stories I told. Over the next 90 minutes, he interrupted colleagues (and me) repeatedly in mid-sentence, dismissed points he disagreed with as "naïve" or "idiotic," openly questioned the competence of several members of his team, made nasty comments about their personal appearance (telling one she was too short and another he needed to lose weight) — and when he wasn't talking, he was focused on his BlackBerry. He answered phone calls perhaps three times during the workshop and engaged in one loudly whispered three-minute call as I was trying to present. When the workshop ended, the boss thanked me and bragged about how lucky his people were because — I'm not kidding — he had listened so well, encouraged them to argue with him, and treated them with respect! That guy was living in a fool's paradise, and everyone in the room knew it — except him.*

*... [T]his CEO's lack of self-awareness is something I've witnessed repeatedly. [A] growing pile of research implies that such delusions become even more pronounced when ... bosses feel ... powerful.*[5]

---

5   fastcompany.com/1821051/are-you-a-power-poisoned-boss

Most of you couldn't behave this boorishly if you tried. Please don't try.

Remember: *executive power* has nothing to do with *executive presence*. When you hand an impressive title and responsibilities to a jackass, you're still left with a jackass.

## Business Etiquette for Job Seekers

One of the most important circumstances in which first impressions are most vital is when you interview for a new job. How you perform during a job interview can dictate your career path for the next several years. So, before your next interview, learn how to make a great first impression — and a lasting impression — by reviewing the following tips:

### Job Interview Etiquette Basics:

- Firm "web-to-web"[6] handshake;

- Confident, friendly smile;

- Direct eye-to-eye contact ("eye connection");

- Sit only when asked;

- Offer a copy of your résumé;

- Pace yourself;

- Don't interrupt the interviewer;

- Thank interviewers for their time;

- Follow up immediately.

---

6   The web of your hand is the space (or skin) between your thumb and index finger.

Be aware of the time without ever looking at your watch. Just ask, "Are we doing okay on time?"

| DO: | DON'T: |
|---|---|
| • Look your absolute best | • Fidget, touch their desk |
| • Smile | |
| • Maintain eye contact | • Shake your leg, flick hair, sniff, scratch |
| • Sit up straight | |
| • Slightly lean forward in chair | • Yawn, look at watch at anytime |
| • Acknowledge all interviewers | • Slouch, lean back, cross arms/legs |
| • Look for a clock in the room | • Smoke, chew gum, swear or use slang |
| • Nod when appropriate | • Stare, look too serious |
| • Be concise and don't ramble | • Make any bodily noises |
| • Arrive 5-10 minutes early | • Appear overly nervous, rushed |
| • Give good firm handshake | |

# The Art of Interview Follow-Up

Once you have made a great first impression during your job interview, it is then essential to create a lasting impression, too. The best — and most simple way — is to follow-up on your interview. This helps you achieve top of mind awareness with your interviewer. Use the tips that follow to ensure you are remembered long after the interview is over.

### Make Use of Interviewer's Business Card

- Use correct titles;

- Correct spelling of interviewer names;

- Correct street addresses.

### Send Thank-You Note

- Send note within 24 hours;

- Use your best judgment re: mail or email;

- Text must be 100% accurate;

- Send to all interviewers;

- Send after every interview;

- Show appreciation for the company's interest in you;

- Restate your interest in job and company;

- Restate your qualifications for the position;

- Include your contact references:

    o Call all of your references to inform them that they may be contacted by the company;

    o Tell them about the position for which you interviewed, so they can speak to your strengths.

### Make Follow-up Call

- Call 5 to 7 days after the interview;

- If possible, avoid calling on Mondays; interviewers are more likely to be busy;

- Be brief and concise;

- Be patient;

- Do not call back more than 3 times.

# Assessment Exercise

1. Which character traits or competencies do you think people associate with you? Which others would you add?

2. Which negative attributes or habits do you think people associate with you? Do you consider these negative or is it just that others do?

3. Make a quick list of your social identities (you have more than one). Which of these is your choice to emphasize into your *workplace* interactions?

4. Which perception of you held by others do you care about? Which do you not care about?

5. Of all the people you interact with in any way, which five people count most with you? How would *they* describe you?

# Protect Your Online Image

## CHAPTER EIGHT

As a rule, I recommend that you never post anything online that you wouldn't want to see on a billboard outside your CEO's office. Establishing and maintaining a professional virtual image requires that you do more than just align your online image with your offline image. You must work *harder* to create and protect a virtual image and reputation — if only because the Internet offers very few iron-clad privacy guarantees. Anything you type in an email or post to a social media site may eventually be viewed by someone in a position to make or break your career and your reputation.

Chances are, your friends will never share the tasteless joke you made about the boss over drinks the other night. Posting that same joke to a social media site, however, could land you in the unemployment line if the boss ever sees it. And by now, you should know that incidents like this are not just the stuff of urban legend — they are everyday events. The media is filled with stories of job candidates who lost promising opportunities because company HR directors located compromising Facebook photos of them — photos showing them half-dressed and bleary-eyed at a booze-fueled bacchanal. There are numerous reports of employees who were fired after management uncovered unflattering or indiscreet comments that they'd made via email or in a chat room.

Whether or not you believe it is "fair" for management to monitor employees' Internet habits or judge job candidates based on youthful indiscretions is not the point. To quote Peter O'Toole in *Lawrence of Arabia*: "What's fair got to do with it?" This is how the business world works. What happens in Vegas might *not* actually stay in Vegas. Your personal image will spill over into your workplace image — if you allow it. You will be judged (sometimes) for your offsite behavior because some managers and clients believe that how we conduct our personal lives reflects how we conduct our professional lives.

Because of this, one of my most sacred rules for protecting a virtual image is to keep your personal and professional lives separate.

## Put a Divider between Work and Home

Without question, the Internet is a fantastic tool for building and enhancing an image. You can quickly establish yourself as a thought leader on a specific topic, expanding your reputation and increasing your visibility through websites, blogs, videos, tweets and texts. Now more than ever, it is easy to position yourself as a credible expert. But it is also easier than ever to create a reputation that positions you as incompetent, untrustworthy, unreliable and unintelligent, especially if you use email and social media to denigrate your superiors, peers and customers — and even if you merely engage in "harmless" celebrity gossip. If the wrong people discover that you've been tweeting nasty rumors or posting inappropriate pictures on Facebook, your carefully woven image could unravel overnight.

There is no clear-cut dividing line between the online and offline worlds. There are also few clear-cut boundaries between the office and home. The boundaries have become very permeable — home phone numbers were once reserved for family and friends, and colleagues were expected to call *only* in the event of an emergency, but today's salespeople and account executives hand out their personal phone numbers like Halloween candy. What once demonstrated someone's commitment to 24/7 customer service has become so commonplace that it is now expected, which has helped blur the lines between work and home — not to mention business hours and leisure hours. Thanks to cell phones and the Internet, the professional and social worlds have merged.

Take Facebook as an example. Many Facebook users have no problem friending any colleague who wants to be friended. So when Sally posts pictures from her weekend pool party, she is *inviting* her work colleagues to become part of her personal life. She's asking them to cross the boundary between the professional and the personal — even the intimate. Millions of people do this every day without realizing that they are blurring the lines between work and home. Privacy settings on social media sites, particularly on Facebook, are not dependable and are constantly changing.

You should be very selective about which colleagues (if any) you invite into your personal space — online *and* offline personal space. Sad to say, but I know a number of people whose private criticisms of management were revealed to management by seemingly trustworthy colleagues. George once lost a job when one of his closest work friends told a supervisor about some unflattering comments George had made. This "friend" had been working on contract for the company, but was expecting to be made a permanent employee. When she confided in George that she was so confident about being hired that she was going to buy a new house, George warned her to hold off on the purchase. "I would not trust Susan as far as I could throw her," he said. Within two weeks, George went from being an "indispensable man" at the company to an unemployed man.

If this sort of thing can happen between "friends" who work face-to-face on a daily basis, just imagine what could happen if a rival or an enemy got hold of inappropriate information you've posted to Facebook or a confidential email between you and another colleague. What if you accidentally sent an email to everyone in the division instead of just the intended recipient(s)? It happens.

Be very careful about giving your work friends the same access to personal information that you give to personal friends — information you wouldn't want just anyone to see. If you have good rapport with someone, and they are a reliable friend, you're probably okay. At a minimum, however, don't share anything privately with colleagues that you wouldn't share in the cafeteria or at the water cooler.

The lines between your personal and professional lives can become so fuzzy that the potential for mayhem increases exponentially. The knowledge you share with colleagues and clients can feed into office politics and fuel interpersonal dramas. Someone might friend you on Facebook, extract personal information, and then use it against you later to gain favor in the office.

I'm not trying to work you into a state of paranoia, but it's important to remember that information is power. The moment you let someone enter your personal domain, you are giving him leverage over you in the workplace. Be careful.

Social media is being used more and more to weed out job applicants — to learn more about their background and character. Social media essentially erases the line between professional and private worlds. The best way to stay out of trouble is to develop a consistent policy for using social media and the Internet.

For example, my policy is to *never* accept as Facebook friends people with whom I work directly. No exceptions. Some of my colleagues have asked if they could friend me on Facebook, but I have politely declined. I explain that I use Facebook only for family and friends with whom I don't work directly. Sometimes I'll also say, "I like to keep my work life and my personal life separate" and/or "I reserve Facebook interactions for family and non-work friends."

Social media sites are continually changing their policies, and most of us don't take the time to familiarize ourselves with the changes. We don't keep up with the changes because they're making them every other day, it seems. But it's important to be aware of these changes, particularly those that affect privacy settings.

> If you don't want to create a policy that's as restrictive as mine, consider creating compartmentalized groups — e.g., a group called Coworkers or Work Friends. You can establish groups like these for work friends versus family versus non-work friends, and create different settings so that members of one

group cannot see certain posts or can't see what people post on your wall. Take advantage of the different ways to control the information that different people see. Build barriers to maintain a veil of separation between work and home.

You may worry about offending people by saying, "I'm not going to friend you." It *can* be a little offensive. It is like refusing to give your cell phone number to someone you've just met — someone with whom you've been enjoying a friendly chat. You don't know the person very well, so it shouldn't be surprising that you don't want to hand out your phone number. On the other hand, it has become so common for people to exchange personal contact information without regard to the length or nature of the relationship that some people *will* take offense if you hesitate to grant them access to your personal domain. You can solve this dilemma by granting them access to selected *portions* of your domain, but not the inner sanctum.

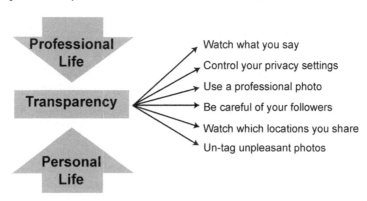

**Figure 5: Separating your personal life from your work life.**

Separating your personal life from your work life is critical to building and maintaining executive presence. It is very difficult to build executive presence if you are continually blurring the line between the personal and professional. When the issue arises of granting access to your personal life, the most important thing to consider is "Does this person need to know this? Do I want this degree of familiarity with this person?"

I don't necessarily want the people who report to me to know what I do on the weekends. It's not that I have anything to hide, it's just none of their business. My secretary and other direct staff don't need to know where I live, which restaurants I frequent or the names of my friends. Sharing this information can detract from my professional presence by removing some of the mystique that surrounds my position and authority.

Having an executive presence doesn't mean you have to project it 24/7. You may not want to be "on" during your leisure time. We all have flaws and idiosyncrasies that we need to minimize during business hours to maintain professional presence and/or executive presence. Fortunately, if we keep work separate from our personal lives, we can relax during our down time, and not worry about our "warts" showing. However, if we grant colleagues access to our personal lives, we may feel the need to stay "on" after business hours.

If you've ever run into your boss on the street over the weekend and were surprised at how he was dressed and the people he was with, you know what I mean. It can come as a shock to see how the boss dresses and comports himself outside a professional setting because his professional image is the only image you've ever seen.

# Image Management

## CHAPTER NINE

Enhancing your image requires a plan. It also requires time, patience and a real desire to project a better image over the long haul. Image enhancement starts with *awareness* of the need to change, followed by an *understanding* of what needs to change. From there, you'll need to translate *desires* into corresponding *actions*, including image maintenance (once you have achieved your short-term goals).

To succeed in this journey, you'll need a roadmap and an image team to help you navigate the process and to consistently project that image. The last thing you want is to backslide into old habits or wander into uncharted territory without a guide.

Although your image team can help you create a customized plan, every roadmap should contain some variation on the following steps.

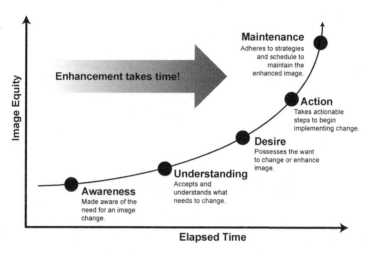

**Figure 6: Image enhancement begin with awareness.**

**Build a personal image management team:** Assemble a team to help you achieve objectives regarding your physical appearance, your style-related behaviors, and your communication style. The team may include, but does not have to be limited to, a personal trainer, dentist, nutritionist, hair stylist, image consultant and a business coach. Your team's mission is to help you look, feel and be your best. Make a list of your current team; identify any gaps and then fill them. Set a regular schedule to meet separately with each expert.

**Solicit objective feedback on your current image:** Hire a consultant or ask someone you trust to provide feedback on your image: your dress, actions, language, written communications and business etiquette. Identify areas that aren't aligned with how you wish to present yourself, especially those that create a negative perception. Focus on improving negative image traits. They have more power to damage your image than positive traits have to improve it.

**Focus on appearance first:** Because first impressions are so important to business interactions, focus on your dress and grooming first. People form impressions of you and your abilities based on how you package yourself. When in doubt, overdress. It is easier to "dress down" after creating a good first impression than it is to "dress up" to regain lost ground.

**Evaluate and upgrade your wardrobe and style:** Dressing well forces people to stop and take notice, giving you the opportunity to prove your abilities. At least once a year, conduct a wardrobe review that evaluates fit, wear and tear, and current style, and replace any pieces that do not convey your desired image. You can upgrade your style very quickly with a new haircut or a new pair of stylish glasses.

**Understand the psychological impact of colors:** Color plays a critical role in the way others perceive you. As a rule, wear darker colored clothing when you want to be perceived as credible or authoritative. Wear lighter colored clothing, textured fabrics, and unmatched suits when you want to be perceived as more friendly. Consult an expert in color analysis to help you identify the colors that complement the undertones of your skin.

**Maintain a neat workspace:** Your office or cubicle says a lot about the way you think, work and manage. Disorganized and cluttered workspaces create perceptions of someone who is not in control — not even of himself. Neat, clean and organized workspaces create perceptions of someone who is structured, thorough and logical. Take five minutes daily, including before meetings, to tidy and organize your workspace.

**Monitor your digital image:** Clients and colleagues will form impressions that either elevate or erode your credibility based on your digital image. You should regularly search your name online to stay aware of what others might see about you.

Develop a personal policy regarding the people who will be included in your social media sphere. If you want to leverage social media, but don't want to share personal information, create both public and private profiles.

**Align every aspect of your brand:** The goal of a brand is to create a consistent image in the minds of your peers and clients. If your core image is "conservative" or "creative," this should be reflected in your dress, actions, language, written communications and business etiquette. Avoid appearances and behaviors that send inconsistent or incongruent messages. An expensive suit worn with old unshined shoes and careless grooming will send the message that you don't care about the details. Make sure that all aspects of your appearance are polished and impeccable.

# Don't Overspend

Image management doesn't have to be expensive. The point is not to spend beyond your means, hoping your new image will pay for itself before your creditors catch up with you. Nobody expects you to dress like the CEO of a Fortune 500 company on an assistant's salary. Image enhancement *can* be affordable. In fact, image enhancement *must* be affordable, or the image you project may not be congruent with who you really are — and your current job status is part of who you really are. The entry-level employee who stocks her closet with $50,000 worth of designer fashions is more likely to evoke suspicion and envy than executive presence. I've encountered many people who dressed beyond their means, and my first impression was usually not "What an impressive, well-dressed person." More often than not, my impression was "How can she afford to wear those outfits? Does she have a trust fund, did she marry into money or max out her credit cards? Does she even need to work for a living?"

Before hiring an image consultant, do some research, prioritize your goals, and create a reasonable budget. You might not be able to accomplish every goal in one fell swoop. You might have to first make sure you have the right hairstyle and the right makeup. (And when I talk about the "right" makeup, I mean colors that match your skin's undertones, hair color, eye color, etc.) You might start by simply buying a new pair of glasses and two or three new suits. Again, it is best to launch an image enhancement program by first focusing on your appearance, since how you look makes the greatest initial impression on other people. Focus on visual appearance first, and then expand the program to include communication style, etiquette and digital image. Take an inventory of what is working for you and what is not. Then prioritize the changes that you want to make according to the impact they have on others.

There is no shortage of image consultants working in almost every conceivable field related to visual image, communication and etiquette. You can hire an image consultant to help you determine what colors are best for you, to perform a body-type analysis or a facial analysis. You can hire a consultant to conduct a wardrobe assessment. You can even hire people to do your clothes shopping for you. Some people hate shopping so much that they hire experts to escort them through stores, so that they won't buy the first thing they see on a mannequin — just to get it over with.

There are etiquette coaches who will help you with your business etiquette, as well as help with cross-cultural etiquette. Hire an expert to help with whatever your goals are. There are many ways to leverage their services; you can use them for a one-time evaluation, occasionally as needed, or on a retainer basis. You can tackle every image gap at one time or work through your program in phased steps. It all depends on your priorities and budget.

## The Authentic Self Will Always Prevail

Image management can go only so far because all of us project our external image from within. Although part of image enhancement involves camouflaging visual weaknesses, it is not possible — nor desirable — to camouflage your authentic self. That self will always prevail in the end, no matter how hard you might try to mask it. And why would you want to mask it? If you have a genuine desire to hide your true self from others, image enhancement is not the correct path to follow at this time — a therapist, spiritual counselor or self-improvement program might be in order. It is not possible to project executive presence if you are not happy with your authentic self. High self-esteem (but not egotism) is the very foundation on which executive presence is built.

This doesn't mean that you must be born a flawless exemplar of all that is good and noble and virtuous. Memorable leaders are made, not born. In fact, one of history's greatest leaders was very much a self-made man when it came to image — an image he self-consciously cultivated over an entire lifetime.

George Washington was neither a demigod nor (as some revisionist historians would have you believe) a lucky incompetent born with a silver spoon in his mouth. He was a *very* self-aware individual who devoted much of his life to overcoming his self-perceived flaws. More than any other

Founding Father, he was aware that every word he spoke and every action he undertook would be recorded for posterity and scrutinized by historians. Washington was keenly aware that he was the *role-model-in-chief* for the new nation and, as such, that he needed to project executive presence. He did everything he could to project such an image.

He was not born a leader, but he deliberately crafted himself into one. He even used his flaws — vanity, ambition, a fierce temper and an obsession with his personal reputation — as raw materials from which he later constructed the image of a wise and visionary leader. By continuously recognizing and learning from his mistakes (often hard and bloody mistakes), he strove to remake himself into a more noble, more enlightened man.

As a boy, Washington hand-copied the *Rules of Civility & Decent Behavior*, a Jesuit guide to gentlemanly conduct. The book guided his conduct for the rest of his life. Though some of the book's admonitions seem trite ("Put not off your Cloths in the presence of Others, nor go out your Chamber half Dressed") or even oddball ("Spit not in the Fire, nor Stoop low before it neither Put your Hands into the Flames to warm them, nor Set your Feet upon the Fire especially if there be meat before it"), other precepts stressed what we now call "social skills."

In addition, Washington chose as his role models some of the most virtuous men of classical history, including the Roman statesman Cato. He was especially fond of a play about Cincinnatus, the Roman farmer who left his plow to lead an army that saved Rome. Following his victory, Cincinnatus returned to his farm, refusing the role of dictator offered by the Senate.

Ironically, the greatest test of Washington's leadership took place not on the battlefield, but well after the British defeat at Yorktown. In March 1783, some of Washington's most trusted officers conspired to overthrow the new national government in a military coup. The crisis reached a boiling point on March 11, when rebellious officers scheduled a meeting to coordinate their strategy. Washington countermanded the order, and scheduled a meeting for March 16. In the hours before the assembly, Washington struggled to write a speech that would dissuade his disaffected brethren from pursuing this course — a course that had crushed so many republics before, and would cause so many later revolutionaries to abandon promises of liberty and equality. The dream of American democracy was something very personal to Washington. He made that clear in his address, telling his officers that he would view a betrayal of the Revolution's ideals as a personal betrayal.

Washington won over his officers before he even began the speech. In a theatrical gesture that has since become legendary, he set his notes before him on the lectern and paused, reaching into his pocket to produce a pair of glasses. "Gentlemen, you will permit me to put on my spectacles" he declared rhetorically, "for I have not only grown gray but almost blind in service to my country."[1] Within moments, there wasn't a dry eye in the house.

Like his hero Cincinnatus, George Washington refused the mantle of a Caesar when it was proffered, choosing to cast aside self-interest. "Upon learning that Washington intended to reject the mantle of emperor, no less a figure than King

---

1    Ellis, Joseph J., Founding Brothers. New York: Alfred A. Knopf, 2001, p. 130.

George III is said to have observed, "If he does that, he will be the greatest man in the world."[2]

You could have no better role model than George Washington.

The ultimate goal of image enhancement is to bring the inner and outer image into perfect synchronization — to ensure that the inner self and outer self are harmonious and balanced. To achieve this, your external image should reflect the way you live and work — with personal integrity, high professional standards and an inviolable code of honor.

---

2   Ibid.

# About the Author

*David A. McKnight* is a style icon in the making. He began his career in 1996 as a management consultant for Ernst & Young after completing his MS in Public Policy and Management at Carnegie Mellon University. Prior to graduate school, David studied sociology and philosophy at Rutgers University, and completed a fellowship in Public Policy Analysis at Princeton University.

David began DAMstyle, an exclusive image and lifestyle consulting enterprise, in 2006 as a way to fulfill his personal passion for style. Since the company's debut, David swiftly made his mark as a published stylist and certified image consultant, simultaneously building an impressive roster of high-profile clients and achievements. Among his notable achievements, David has served as the creative director of an online magazine; styled celebrities for magazine photo shoots; wrote and published image articles; managed and styled numerous fashion shows during New York's Fashion Week;

hosted an online fashion reality show; judged the Miss Teen New York pageant; served as the Men's Editor of a popular online fashion-luxury magazine; and also briefly filled the role of Image Director at Career Gear, a non-profit organization that provides a business suit and support to under-served men seeking employment. While working at Deloitte Consulting as a senior manager, David leveraged his expertise to help develop a course component titled "Communicating with Presence and Confidence," which focused on partner development. He also worked on a small committee to develop professional standards for the firm, and delivered several presentations on the topic of professional image at Deloitte University.

When not working with clients, David continues to work in corporate America, within the financial services industry. He currently resides in Manhattan, and in his free time, he delights in running, reading books on business and style, wine tasting, trotting the globe and, of course, shopping.

Made in the USA
Monee, IL
06 September 2020